OUTREACH SERVICES
FOR TEENS

ALA Editions purchases fund advocacy, awareness,
and accreditation programs for library professionals worldwide.

OUTREACH SERVICES FOR TEENS

A STARTER GUIDE

JESS SNOW

FOREWORD BY
ANTHONY BERNIER

ALA Editions
CHICAGO 2020

JESS SNOW is the teen services team leader in Teen Central of the Boston Public Library. She was the first teen outreach librarian for the Oakland Public Library. Snow has established several outreach partners for both the Boston and Oakland libraries and has been providing outreach services for teens since 2003. She has written extensively about outreach, as well as presenting locally and nationally on outreach services to teens. Snow served on the VOYA (Voice of Youth Advocates) Advisory Board and had a regular column in VOYA for more than two years. She also served on the YALSA Board of Directors for two years.

© 2020 by Jess Snow

Extensive effort has gone into ensuring the reliability of the information in this book; however, the publisher makes no warranty, express or implied, with respect to the material contained herein.

ISBN: 978-0-8389-4815-6 (paper)

Library of Congress Cataloging-in-Publication Data

Names: Snow, Jess, 1970- author.
Title: Outreach services for teens : a starter guide / Jess Snow ; foreword by Anthony Bernier.
Description: Chicago : ALA Editions, 2020. | Includes bibliographical references and index. |
   Summary: "This book provides readers with a working definition of outreach services, shares tools to create successful partners, explores what successful outreach service looks like, and examines ways to evaluate outreach services"—Provided by publisher.
Identifiers: LCCN 2020019296 | ISBN 9780838948156 (paper)
Subjects: LCSH: Libraries and teenagers—United States. | Library outreach programs—United States. | Libraries and community—United States. | Young adults› libraries—Activity programs—United States.
Classification: LCC Z718.5 .S655 2021 | DDC 027.4/2—dc23
LC record available at https://lccn.loc.gov/2020019296

Cover design by Alejandra Diaz.
Text design in the Chaparral, Gotham, and Bell Gothic typefaces.

♾ This paper meets the requirements of ANSI/NISO Z39.48-1992 (Permanence of Paper).

Printed in the United States of America

24 23 22 21 20   5 4 3 2 1

Contents

Foreword by Anthony Bernier   *vii*

Acknowledgments   *ix*

Introduction: My Beginnings in Providing Outreach   *xi*

1 | **What Outreach May Look Like**   *1*

2 | **How to Create Partnerships**   *11*

3 | **The Role of Staff in Providing Outreach**   *29*

4 | **How to Identify Goals and Outcomes for Outreach Services**   *41*

5 | **Incorporating Technology into Your Outreach**   *49*

6 | **How to Create a Core Collection for Outreach**   *53*

7 | **Appendix: Resources**   *61*

    OUTREACH PLAN FOR TEEN LIBRARIANS   62

    MEMORANDUM OF UNDERSTANDING (MOU) EXAMPLE   63

    RESTRICTED MATERIALS FOR A JUVENILE DETENTION FACILITY   65

    SURVEY TO GATHER INPUT FROM TEENS IN A JUVENILE DETENTION FACILITY   66

    NATIONAL ORGANIZATIONS SERVING TEENS   68

    SELECTION TOOLS   70

    CORE TITLES FOR TEEN OUTREACH   72

    BOOKTALKS TO HOOK TEENS ON BOOKS   73

    SAMPLE BOOK CHECKOUT SHEET   74

    STAFF TRAINING RESOURCES   75

    HOW TO STAY SAFE IN A PARTNER'S FACILITY   78

    OPEN-SOURCE AND FREE SOFTWARE TO DOWNLOAD   79

Index   *81*

ANTHONY BERNIER

Foreword

We can follow Jess Snow's journey of development, from starting in a new young adult outreach position, through her progressive, dynamic, and bottom-up outreach efforts as the head of young adult services at the Boston Public Library's historic main branch.

Outreach Services for Teens avoids the vague and clichéd notions about outreach that so many librarians encounter in job descriptions and performance evaluations. Snow argues persuasively that youth librarians should take outreach seriously and systematically, and apply a full complement of professional skills, creativity, analysis, and resourcefulness to the conception, delivery, and evaluation of this essential service, which is especially needed by so many communities with marginalized youth.

I am a professor in a large MLIS program, and my students find it difficult to explicitly address the topic of "outreach" because my courses promote evidence-based practices—and outreach, which has been chronically ill-defined and historically under-researched, as Snow is wise to point out, is not one of these. But it came as a surprise to Snow early in her career, as doubtless it bewilders many other new professionals, that her position required many responsibilities without serious preparation for how to meet the needs of young library users through outreach efforts.

Among the most important and innovative contributions that *Outreach Services for Teens* makes to our professional literature is its comprehensive treatment of the service power that outreach efforts can deliver. Snow articulates the reasons why librarians must take outreach efforts to young adults more seriously, and she builds upon the systematic everyday planning that is required. Readers will benefit tremendously from the many workaday examples of well-executed outreach efforts described in this book.

Overall, Snow advocates constant on-the-job experimentation and testing rather than holding up impossible or vague standards. Beyond that, *Outreach Services for Teens* shows how outreach efforts require articulating clear expectations among and between all stakeholders, and it urges successful practitioners to take up the trainer's mantle and help lead other staff members through these developmental steps.

For all those librarians, middle-managers, and administrators who are wandering around in the wilderness of "outreach" ambiguity, Jess Snow's book offers a clear way forward through the fog and into the bright daylight of thoughtful and professional volition in developing powerful outreach efforts.

So pick up, read, and *use* this copy of *Outreach Services for Teens*. Let Jess Snow lead you through the development of professional efforts for the youth that need them.

Acknowledgments

To Anthony Bernier, MLIS, PhD, and Shelley Quezada, MLIS, my advisors on this project. Thank you for your insight and your valuable perspective on teen services and outreach services, respectively. Your help was critically important to this project.

To my editor, Mardi Chalmers, MLIS, thank you for your discerning eye and brain.

I have had a great opportunity to work with a truly amazing librarian; Ally Dowds, who started at the beginning, conceiving, developing, and implementing outreach and the eventual evaluation of such. To see what she has done has been dazzling.

To Patrick Jones, MLIS: I reached out to you initially in 2008 with many questions about outreach services, and you took so much time with me. You shared the work you began and continued while you were at the Hennepin County Library, all of which was invaluable to me.

Thank you to librarians Teresa Allen, Jennifer Bisson, Trixie Dantis, Bernie Farrell, Cindy Hauenstein, Pamela McCarter, Sharon McKellar, Kate McNair, and Emma Willig for your contributions in each chapter. The work you and your libraries are doing is incredible, which is why it needs to be documented in this book.

To so many of the teens I have worked with who have inspired, taught, and schooled me in so much, thank you for your wisdom.

And thank you to Jamie Santoro of ALA Editions for her support.

Introduction
My Beginnings in Providing Outreach

When I began my library career in teen services in 2004, I began immediately by providing outreach. I hadn't taken any coursework in library school that focused specifically on outreach services, so my definition of the term *outreach* was based on articles I had read while in library school. This definition encapsulated my own interest in what I felt was foundational in library services—bringing the library to the people, and widening their access to library materials. There wasn't a course on outreach in my program of study, and outreach was only briefly mentioned. So I learned about outreach by some failures and a few successes. The successes came later.

As a teen services librarian, I started by reaching out to organizations that I felt served underrepresented teens, talking about the library's services and suggesting ways in which we could possibly partner. Everything I did initially wasn't at all systematic or well thought out. I had no identifying goals and outcomes (I barely knew what those meant).

The first big partnership I established was with the Department of Youth Services (DYS), the Massachusetts state agency that serves incarcerated teens. This didn't happen overnight. It took months before I was able to connect with someone at DYS who took the time to understand what I was trying do with underrepresented teens. I already knew that the Boston Public Library (BPL) didn't offer any services to the three locations and nine units of the Metro Boston area DYS, but I didn't know if other libraries were involved with that department. When I finally connected with the right person, we met and talked about what the library could offer to DYS, and I learned what the department didn't have access to. They had no access to library services.

At the BPL my job title was teen librarian, and while it was in my job description to provide outreach, this wasn't precisely defined for me. Nor was there any time commitment or direction from the library. I was really on my own to figure these out. The DYS and I determined that there would be a need for all nine of its units to receive books every month, and we talked about what that could look like. Should it be simply a book deposit, or would it be a more engaging experience in which the incarcerated teens could have the books described to them before checkout? Yes! That's what was decided. I wrote a proposal to the president of the BPL and outlined what I envisioned this outreach to consist of: one day a month which would take me out of the library completely (meaning I would not be able to staff a desk); prep time to gather books; check them out on an institution library card; create a checkout list of books for incarcerated teens; and finally, get to know the books myself and prepare booktalks. I came up with a total of two days a month that I would need "off desk" and out of the library: one day to prepare each month's visit, and another day to visit the incarceration facilities. I included in the proposal that each year I would present both the president of the library and the DYS with a report containing statistics on the usage of the books checked out and the number of teens I had seen each month. The proposal was approved.

I began my outreach efforts in 2008 with 20 books for each of the nine units—a total of 180 books that I would check out and bring to DYS, as well as giving a booktalk. I would pack up a library car with bags for each of the units and started that way. That first year was a learning curve. The day for the visits began at 8:00 a.m. and ended at 3:30 p.m. Then I would drive back to the library with books that hadn't been checked out. Then I prepared a master file of all the books that got checked out, what unit they went to, and who checked them out. This was a long day, but it was incredibly rewarding. Teens liked to see the books that were brought in and talked about. Most of the teens were readers already, so it was good for them to hear about books they may not have known about. We also talked about the books they were reading. These conversations were helpful in giving me ideas about what books to bring in next. Every month, more and more teens would check out books. As the library began to be a consistent fixture in their days, they began to expect my visits and even requested specific books. By the end of that first year I decided to make some changes to the program:

- Select 10 books for each of the 9 units instead of 20. Twenty books were too many books for each unit, and there were too many booktalks.
- Create an MOU (memorandum of understanding) containing a definition of the program and the responsibilities of each organization.

- Increase the number of librarians providing this service.
- Create a survey for teens participating in the program, to get their feedback.
- Add summer programming or reading programs in DYS.
- Provide library cards for teens, ready to be used when they leave DYS.

By year two of the program, there were three teen librarians participating, making a total of four of us. We arranged it so that each month two of us went to DYS. It just naturally happened that the branch libraries whose teen librarians worked in our DYS program supported the work being done. This was due partly to my sharing the results of the program annually with the president of BPL, which promoted the partnership in a more systematic way. I shared information with other BPL teen librarians who were not involved with the program, as well as putting the word out in the internal staff news. In addition, the changes I wanted to create occurred, so I really began to shape the program in a better way. The survey we created gave a voice to the teens and enabled them to share their thoughts on the program: whether they felt it was beneficial, and if not, why.

The MOU allowed each organization to take responsibility for specific items, and the partners knew exactly what those items were. Having more teen librarians participating allowed for a more diverse staff providing outreach, as well as connecting more library services to DYS. Providing library cards meant that those teens leaving DYS had a solid understanding of what the library provides and a means to access those services. The summer reading/programming continued services in the summer, which nurtured a connection to the library outside of DYS. Most of my learning about outreach took place at DYS; it wasn't something I learned from reading a book or taking a course. It was truly on the job.

Outreach Services for Teens is a guide for teen librarians who want to know more about outreach services to teens and how to advocate for, organize, and provide those services. This book provides details on outreach practices and provides real-life examples of them. Outreach is something that libraries and librarians have been providing outside of public libraries since youth services began. While the job descriptions of many teen and youth services librarians may include "provide outreach" and they are expected to do so, their own libraries are often unable to offer any definition of what outreach is, how to provide it, how to tie outreach into the library's strategic plan, and so on.

This book also offers a working definition of what *outreach services* means, since there isn't a universally accepted definition. For teen librarians as well as library administrators, there needs to be a universally accepted definition of what *outreach* means. Without this standardized definition, there will be confusion about what teen librarians are providing and to whom.

The initial questions for this book were: what is the definition of *outreach*, and how do we provide it to teens? How *outreach* is defined varies from library to library. It can even vary from teen librarian to teen librarian. I read a PhD thesis with the following quote: "While the term outreach is used extensively in library literature from the mid-sixties on, a specific definition is not readily offered. Outreach is often used interchangeably with the synonym 'extension of services' and the phrases 'service to the disadvantaged' or 'unserved,' and 'community' or 'inner-city service.'"[1] While public libraries have been providing outreach services since youth services (mainly a focus on children's services) became more defined in the 1930s, this statement reiterates the lack of a universally accepted definition of *outreach*.

The programs and the services outlined in this book have been used in libraries across the country, but are by no means intended to be replicated unchanged. You should rather think of this book as a guide, a start, and a resource to help you begin providing outreach services to teens.

NOTE

1. Kathleen Weibel, "The Evolution of Library Outreach 1960–75 and Its Effect on Reader Services: Some Considerations," 1982, https://core.ac.uk/download/pdf/4813998.pdf.

1
What Outreach May Look Like

Outreach is difficult to define. The term has been used to describe librarians visiting schools; it's used with marketing; and it is seen on university campuses where outreach librarians "reach out" to a library's patrons to actively educate them about the services a library has to offer. The ALA's Office for Diversity, Literacy, and Outreach Services (ODLOS) defines *outreach* as "providing library services and programs outside the walls of the library to underserved and underrepresented populations; populations such as new and non-readers, LGBT people, people of color, poor and homeless people, and people who are incarcerated." When perusing the articles that have been written about outreach, I found the ODLOS definition to be the most widely used one by them, and the definition's enumeration of the target populations for outreach is also widely accepted. Accordingly, the ODLOS definition of *outreach* is what will be used in this book. Furthermore, ODLOS actively works across the ALA's organizations and membership to consult, facilitate, coordinate, and train librarians, libraries, librarianship, and the library community on issues of equity, diversity, and inclusion.

A SHORT HISTORY OF OUTREACH SERVICES

Historically, underserved populations have been defined as those who have been denied full and equal participation in the economic, social, and institutional activities of society (Civil Rights Act, 1964). Historically, populations have been underserved because of their racial or ethnic background, their geographic location, or their special needs. They have faced such barriers as inability to speak English, physical or mental disabilities, lack of permanent residency or citizenship status, illiteracy, low literacy rates, and age. Underserved populations have variously been identified as poor, needy, culturally deprived, underprivileged, disadvantaged, and, more recently, diverse. Since these populations are often marginalized and underserved, it is crucial for libraries to recognize these populations and provide services and programs to them where they are.

Library outreach services have existed formally since at least the early twentieth century. Formally, because at that time libraries began to see a need for serving populations that were remote, isolated, and unable to get to the library. The idea of bringing books to patrons caught on in the United States, spurred by a widely distributed population and the desire for civic improvement. An influx in public funds from the Works Progress Administration during the Great Depression, especially in the South, led to a surge in library outreach initiatives, including bookmobiles.

In 1901, the librarian Mary Lemist Titcomb of the Washington County Free Library in Hagerstown, Maryland, began a mobile library using a horse-drawn wagon. She set up book-deposit stations in remote rural areas so patrons could access the library's books. After four years, there were sixty-six such stations. Titcomb undertook these new and innovative services because she knew patrons outside of the library who were unable to get to the library and its resources. Her focus on reaching underserved populations and her strategic way of doing so was noticed by the board of trustees at the Washington County Free Library, and they provided funding for an additional wagon to begin providing mobile services. In the first six months of additional funding of this mobile outreach, a total of 1,008 volumes were distributed. For five years, this was the mode of services until an accident destroyed the wagon and the horses went missing. By then, as automobiles were beginning to be ubiquitous, the trustees provided funds for a car, as they saw the great need for continuing outreach services to remote and underserved populations.

Around 1903, the People's Free Library of Chester County, South Carolina, used a mule-drawn wagon to carry wooden boxes of books to the county's more isolated areas. By the 1930s, they were using a bookmobile. Bookmobiles brought books to areas that were remote and hard to get to, and whose folks found it challenging to make the journey to the library. Since these times, bookmobiles and direct-delivery outreach services have continued to be an integral, vital part of libraries around the country. For over 100 years, bookmobiles have served rural, urban, suburban, and tribal areas, bringing access to information and lifelong learning resources to all classes and communities.

The ALA's Committee on Library Extension was established in 1925 to extend library services to unserved areas in the United States. The ALA's focus was on issues related to rural libraries, particularly in the South. In 1926, it issued a report which stated that over 50 million Americans, almost half the population at the time, lacked access to local public libraries. About 93 percent of these Americans lived in "open country" or in small communities with a population of less than 2,500. More than 7 million Black Americans, or 89 percent of the total then living in the South, did not have access to library services. The percentages of the total population in the Southeast without access to public libraries ranged from 56 percent in Florida to 83 percent in Mississippi.

While bookmobiles focused initially on rural and remote areas, later they also focused on urban areas. In 1939–40 the Work Projects Administration began funding library projects, covering the costs of books, salaries, and vehicles, and again bookmobile service expanded. During World War II, bookmobiles had to cope with a rubber shortage for tires, since new tires were limited to essential military needs only.

Delivering library outreach services to American Indian populations has always been a challenge. The Four Corners Mobile Library Project began in 1970 with one bookmobile that served the Navajo and Hopi reservations. A second vehicle was added in 1972. Even though serving American Indian populations was the primary goal, the bookmobiles stopped at a variety of isolated pockets in northern Arizona. The trucks visited not only Indian reservations, colleges, and boarding schools, but also trading posts, post offices, and public health stations. At some of the stops, such as ranger stations, colleges, and chapter houses, the vehicles routinely dropped off a deposit collection. By 1972 the two bookmobiles had a combined total of eighty-five stops, some of them accessible only by dirt road. Eventually, however, these bookmobiles were phased out, and it wasn't until the late 1970s, with acts like the Indian Self-Determination and Education Assistance Act (1975), the National Indian Omnibus Library Bill (1978), and the White House Pre-Conference on Indian Library and Information Services on or Near Reservations (1978), that a movement for the funding of library outreach services to Indians took root.

Pura Belpré needs to be mentioned here, as she worked directly with the Puerto Rican community, bringing the New York Public Library (NYPL) to them. In the 1920s, she became the first Puerto Rican librarian in New York City. Pioneering library outreach programs within the Puerto Rican community, Belpré worked tirelessly in southwest Harlem to institute bilingual story hours, build Spanish-language book collections, and create cultural events. Through her efforts, the 115th Street Branch Library became a cultural center for the Latino community of New York, hosting evenings with well-known figures such as Diego Rivera. In the 1940s and 1950s Belpré devoted herself to writing, but she returned to the NYPL as the Spanish children's specialist in the 1960s. In 1968, she established the South Bronx Library Program to promote library use and services within the Latino community.

During most of the history of outreach, libraries didn't capture statistics that differentiated between children and teens, so the number served by teen outreach services is difficult to estimate. It wasn't until the early 1970s that libraries began to gather separate data about children's and teens' services.

ADVOCATING FOR TEEN OUTREACH SERVICES

Before understanding more about outreach, an expanded list of just who the "underserved and underrepresented" populations are is needed. It is the responsibility of a democratic society to serve and support the following groups and individuals, including teen populations within those groups:

- Historically disadvantaged racial groups
- Those discriminated against based on their gender or sexual identity, orientation, or expression
- Those from other protected classes, including age, religion, and disability status
- Those discriminated against based on their ethnicity or language
- Those who experience socioeconomic barriers
- People who are geographically isolated
- People who are experiencing food insecurity, homelessness, or poverty
- Immigrants, refugees, and new Americans
- Teens who are, or were, incarcerated
- New and non-readers

The goal of outreach is to extend the services of the physical, brick-and-mortar library to members of the demographics listed above. The need for these services is especially great within the teen population, as we can see by the figures below.

The data on underserved teen populations is astounding. In 2015, there were about 48,000 juveniles incarcerated in the United States at any one time.[1] Almost all of these youth will reenter the community after completing their sentences. The Point in Time Estimates of Homelessness (a count of sheltered and unsheltered homeless persons on a single night in January) in 2017 counted 40,800 unaccompanied youth living in shelters or on the streets. In 2017, more than 690,000 children and teens spent time in foster care in the United States.[2] On average, youth remain in state care for nearly two years, but 6 percent of the youth in foster care have remained there for five or more years. One-quarter of all youths in the United States are immigrants. Each year the United States admits 75,000 refugees (though during the Trump administration this number decreased to 45,000).[3]

There are many barriers facing potential teen patrons for the public library. Some of these youths may be hindered by a lack of mobility or transportation. Poverty may also be a factor. Moreover, confusion about what a public library provides could also keep teens away from the library. If we want to provide library services and programs to underserved or underrepresented populations, and those who are limited by mobility or poverty, we must go to where the need is. We simply must go to where those populations are. The brick-and-mortar library might reach a percentage of those who live close by, but what about those who live farther away, without transportation? What happens when no public transportation is available? What about those with disabilities? In addition, there are other barriers that keep people from entering libraries. There are barriers of cultural differences, unfamiliarity with English, fears and psychological barriers; or people may be incarcerated, or experiencing homelessness.

These are the same barriers that keep teen populations from the library. The traditional attitude that "the books are in the library, come and get them" has become outdated. You can also think of outreach services as a way to find library patrons you didn't know you had. By providing outreach, you are bringing the library to the people; the services and programs may be abridged, but you are still managing to provide them.

First Steps for Providing Outreach

1. Be clear about what outreach is. In your advocacy for outreach services, you should provide examples of what outreach is, show examples of library systems that are doing it right, and explain how these services can not only benefit out-of-the-library populations, but the physical library as well. In each of the following chapters, there are examples of libraries and library systems which have provided successful and meaningful outreach services. But to advocate for outreach services, you must also have a good sense of who needs your library's services and programs, and where they live in your own community. You must do preliminary research into your city, town, neighborhood, or county and know its population and the organizations which serve that population.

Some library systems like the Brooklyn Public Library (BPL) or the New York Public Library have outreach services departments, but other libraries may expect librarians to provide outreach on the basis of their job description. Some library systems will even have outreach as a focus in their strategic plan, but don't really provide institutional support for consistent and sustainable outreach activities. And since many libraries fail to provide institutional support for it, outreach has often been done in more of a grassroots manner.

One of the three focus areas in the Brooklyn Public Library's strategic plan[4] of 2018 is "focusing on community," that is, recognizing the rich diversity of Brooklyn. Some neighborhoods in the borough have a large population of aging residents and few resources aside from the library to foster lifelong learning. Other neighborhoods have many immigrants with low levels of English-language ability, and not enough support services or English classes for those immigrants. In some neighborhoods, teen programs are in high demand, while in others services for young families are the priority. To become more responsive to the different needs of its varying neighborhoods, the BPL focuses on two things: data-gathering and community engagement. With its strategic plan the library is making a commitment: it is sharing the plan with the public, defining the expectations for its staff, and providing information on return on investment. A lot of us aren't in a situation like this in our libraries, so how do you provide outreach services, advocate for them in your library, and not burn yourself out in doing so at the same time?

2. *Look at the demographics of your city, town, or suburb.* You should carefully examine the demographics of your community. What is the percentage of teens and families living below the poverty line, and of teens born outside of the United States? What is the racial/ethnic makeup and character of the community? You can visit the website of your city, town, or suburb to get a sense of the priorities the mayor and the municipal government have laid out. Do any of those priorities include working with and providing services to people who are homeless, who were previously incarcerated, or who are immigrants or refugees? If this is a focus of the community in which you work, this should be a focus for your library, and this gives your advocacy legs.

3. *Check out the social services organizations in your city.* Does your municipal government have a Department of Children and Families, the agency that serves youth who are in foster care? Is there a juvenile detention facility, and are there organizations that work with previously incarcerated youth? Are there any immigrant services or services for refugees? You can use the resource www.youth.gov to search by "map my community" and your zip code, and then tailor your search to find out about the programs that work with underserved youth in your area.

There are "independent living skills coordinators"[5] in each of the fifty states (housed mostly in capital cities). The Independent Living Skills Program (ILSP) is a federally funded agency designed to assist eligible youth in making successful transitions from foster care to independent living. ILSP coordinators are responsible for helping youth in foster care to access services that will assist them in achieving self-sufficiency prior to exiting foster care. If the state and city where you work has an independent living skills coordinator, you could work with them.

By law, every school district must provide schooling to homeless youth and must provide a liaison for those students. The McKinney-Vento Act[6] is a federal law that provides federal money for homeless shelter programs. Also, all states must designate a statewide homeless coordinator to review policies and create procedures, including dispute resolution procedures, to ensure that homeless children are able to attend school. This means there is a coordinator in your state, whom you can contact when you are beginning to create partnerships to offer library services. Local school districts must appoint "local education liaisons" to ensure that school staffs are aware of these children's rights. These liaisons facilitate homeless children's access to schools and transportation services.

Doing the research into all of what was just listed should give you a comprehensive picture of the youth-related social services that exist in your city, town, or suburb. Showing your library's administration the existing youth-related services in your institution, and then showing them who the library isn't serving, can provide a comprehensive picture of the work that needs to be done and just where the library lacks services.

How can you tie your outreach services into the focus of the community? Your city or town may have a focus on designing services and programs for specific populations. Find out if they do, and then find a contact within the city government to whom you can promote the library's services.

4. *Present your findings to your library's administration.* In your report you should include the following:

- Are you able to tie in outreach services to your library's strategic plan? If so, say so and how. If not, are there other reasons why you and the library should be providing outreach services, based on the demographics in your community?
- Who will be providing outreach from your library? Will it be you or a department, or both?
- Who will you be providing outreach to? Give the names of any organizations you are thinking of partnering with.
- What will be your time commitment for outreach?
- What will your outreach consist of?
- Evaluation. How will you share with the administration the success of the outreach services? What are the deliverables? What are the goals and objectives?

Principles to Apply

- Be creative with the definition of *outreach*. You can use the ODLOS definition of *outreach*, but keep in mind that there is no "one size fits all" mold for what outreach is. The outreach services that one library provides can be very different from those of another library.
- Engage with teens outside of the building. Think about the

populations you are serving and their needs and limitations, knowing that this will assist you in getting outside.

- Engage stakeholders. The library will be providing the outreach, but you need input from the stakeholders as to what that outreach looks like: partner organizations, the teens you're serving, and the library administration and staff.
- Be consistent with the services you are providing. Make a schedule with the partner organization and adhere to it.

INVOLVING LIBRARY STAFF

If your library doesn't have an outreach services department, how do you go about involving other staff in providing outreach? Often in libraries, individual librarians will provide outreach. Sometimes these activities aren't coordinated, and if others in the library are doing outreach, things may get confusing and services duplicated. Part of the issue with individual librarians providing outreach is that often it isn't centrally coordinated, so the administration may not know about the services already being provided. There can be another problem: when only one individual is doing outreach and that employee leaves the library or that position, the outreach services end as well, unfortunately.

Before I established the outreach program at the Boston Public Library in 2008, I reached out to Patrick Jones, who was then the manager of outreach services at the Hennepin County (MN) Public Library. We thoroughly discussed how to begin an outreach program: working with outside partners, looking at the MOUs he had worked on with outside partners, the ways to involve existing staff, and more. These conversations, as well as the resources Patrick provided me with, were extremely helpful when I put together an outreach plan. My 2008 position wasn't as an outreach librarian. As the teen librarian, I wrote up my vision of a partnership with the Department of Youth Services (DYS), the goals of the outreach program, and how much time the program would take me outside of the library. I proposed that I work one seven-hour day each month for prep work, which consisted of gathering books, putting together booktalks, checking books out, and writing up checkout lists for DYS. I would spend another day each month making outreach visits to the nine sites. So this was a total of two days' work each month. My proposal was approved by the administration, and I was given the necessary time to provide outreach to the DYS sites, but this was a significant amount of work for just one person. Some of the duties could easily be delegated to other staff, if they could be found. For one year, I did the program all by myself. I loved it, but it was a lot of work managing the program and providing outreach, all while carrying out the duties of being a teen librarian. So I talked about the program to other teen librarians, and more of them became interested in participating.

By circulating the documents of the program which I had put together, I was able to reduce my time commitment to the program as other librarians began to participate, with the acknowledgement and support of the administration. There were nine units in the DYS, and with two librarians making site visits each month, that split the work in half. This is a good example of how a grassroots program can grow due to increased staff participation. As knowledge of the program spread, more librarians began participating in it. This scalable model also serves as one that could utilize interns or volunteers, or both.

Developing an outreach program on your own can be challenging. But looking at already existing programs and talking to their practitioners can help a lot. Some of the things you may be thinking of have already been created, so you wouldn't be starting from scratch. In terms of staffing, you should think about who works within your own institution and what their specific job descriptions are. But could what you're thinking about doing create additional work for library assistants? If so, that may be something that needs to be worked out with the union. That's okay. If you are thinking about that possibility, it's not a roadblock. It just means you must allow more time for negotiations.

Trying to find staff to provide outreach services can be challenging, in terms of the preconceived notions that some staff have about the teens the outreach program works with. They may have negative views about working with incarcerated teens, and those views may be completely inaccurate. You should be comprehensive in providing information about the specific outreach services the library will provide, and realistic about the populations they will be serving. If you are working with teens who are incarcerated, you will be in a lockdown facility with bars and gates that prevent free traffic throughout the facility. This may be challenging for some staff members. Depending on the services you are providing (books, technology, etc.), you want to have staff who want to work with teens in general. It doesn't matter where those teens are, but it does matter that those staff members are truly comfortable, supportive, and open to working with teens.

Libraries have always served underserved and underrepresented populations. The outreach librarian should have a deep understanding of the community the library serves, know the point of outreach, and advocate for outreach. A good proposal that enumerates the goals of the outreach program is needed, as well as clear objectives and a mechanism for evaluating the effectiveness of the outreach. Involving the right staff can make outreach to underrepresented teens in your community a viable and sustainable service.

NOTES

1. Child Trends, "Key Facts about Juvenile Incarceration," 2016, www.childtrends
   .org/indicators/juvenile-detention.
2. Children's Rights, "Foster Care," www.childrensrights.org/newsroom/
   fact-sheets/foster-care/.
3. Refugee Council USA, "Midyear Refugee Arrivals Report," April 2, 2019, www
   .rcusa.org/blog/mid-year-refugee-arrivals-report.
4. Brooklyn Public Library, "Strategic Plan," www.bklynlibrary.org/strategicplan/
   report#next.
5. Child Welfare Information Gateway, "Information on Independent Living Skills
   Coordinators," www.childwelfare.gov/organizations/?CWIGFunctionsaction
   =rols:main.dspList&rolType=Custom&RS_ID=145.
6. U.S. Department of Education, "McKinney-Vento Act," www.ed.gov/policy/elsec/
   leg/esea02/pg116.html.

REFERENCES

Levinson, Nancy Smiler. "Takin' It to the Streets." *Library Journal*, May 1991.

Mallory, Mary. "The Rare Vision of Mary Utopia Rothrock: Organizing Regional Library Services in the Tennessee Valley." *Library Quarterly: Information, Community, Policy* 65, no. 1 (1995): 62–88

2
How to Create Partnerships

CREATING PARTNERSHIPS

What is your partnership going to look like? Will your library provide services and/or programming consistently for the outreach program? You already know the unique services and programs that your library provides. How can you take those services and programs outside the library and provide them to new or underserved populations? By creating partnerships!

Your research has shown you which populations the library doesn't serve in your community, and you know the organizations that do work with those populations. You should be reaching out to these organizations. Before reaching out to an organization, you will need a sense of the time commitment you'll be able to give to working with that organization (once a week, every month, specific number of hours). Share this with your supervisor to ensure that this is a commitment you will be able to adhere to. You should discuss with the potential partner organization what the library can provide. You could talk briefly about what you already do with other partners. Most important, listen to the people in the organization, and you may discover ways in which you can partner with them. Ask them what teens need from their organization. You may be speaking to adults in the organization, or you may be meeting with the teens themselves. If you are talking directly to teens, again, listening is crucial. Are there barriers you can help break down? Try to help these teens understand the things the library does and what it can provide. Try to align the goals of the library with that of the partner organization; this allows for a shared mission.

When creating a partnership, always think about its sustainability. What will it take to keep the partnership going? How many librarians or departments will be providing outreach in the partnership? Be certain of the time commitment and logistics involved in keeping the partnership an active participation, with each partner contributing equally.

TYPES OF YOUTH FACILITIES

There are several different types of youth facilities you might partner with in your community. Many of these settings don't have library services. The major types are discussed in the sections below.

Homeless Shelters

National estimates show that 1.3 to 1.7 million youth experience one night of homelessness or more each year, with 550,000 youth being homeless for a week or longer. Some cities and towns may have shelters or emergency shelters for youth ages 14–24 or 16–22. There are also family shelters that may include teens. Emergency shelters will provide just that: urgent shelter, usually for a short period until teens can find more permanent housing. Other shelters provide long-term housing for teens. Some teens who access homeless shelters may also be participating in a long-term program where they work with a case manager to reach specific goals, whether those are housing, school, or work. Shelters sometimes provide services for homeless teens like mental health counseling, HiSET (the High School Equivalency Test exam is the new alternative to the GED test) programs, or career or work programs. You should know the shelters in your area and understand what they provide to homeless teens.

Foster Homes

Teens in foster care may live in individual foster homes, therapeutic foster homes (for teens who have difficulties in their ability to function within their own families, in school, or in the community), group homes, or residential facilities. Foster homes can be with a family or with a single person, with the caregiver acting as a parent to that youth for a shorter or longer period. The goal is most often to get that teen back to their biological family, but there may be things the family needs to work on first. This could be an alcohol or drug dependency, anger-management issues, or even more serious situations like abandonment or abuse. The youth in foster care are involved through the state agency usually known as the Department of Children and Families (DCF). There is a main department in every state, and several offices throughout that state's cities and counties. Agencies like the DCF will try to place youths in relatives' homes, but if that's not possible, they will place them with a foster family/parent.

Group Homes

Group homes provide therapy and 24-hour supervision and support to teens (who are either wards of the state, or in foster care) in a home-like setting. Unlike large residential treatment facilities or psychiatric hospitals, group homes serve a small number of teens. They reside in a family-like setting with trained staff. Some of these facilities may have a private or special education school on site. The teens housed in these facilities may have severe learning issues, or are dealing with the effects of abuse and/or neglect. A public school setting probably wouldn't be able to address those needs.

Residential Facilities

Residential facilities may be operated by public or private agencies and often provide an array of youth services, including therapeutic services and family, educational, and medical services for children or youth. Placement in a group or residential care facility should only be considered once community-based services have proven ineffective.

Independent Living Skills Program

The Independent Living Skills Program (ILSP) program exists throughout the United States, one in each state. It teaches teens who are in foster care the skills they will need to take their next steps in life. It used to be that teens in foster care aged out at age 18. However, the Fostering Connections to Success and Increasing Adoptions Act of 2008 stated that youth in foster care up to the age of 21 may remain in foster care by receiving reimbursements for their living expenses and school expenses. Twenty-five of the 50 states now employ this act. Each of the 50 states has an ILSP coordinator. The ILSP program is voluntary for youth aged 16 and older to participate, to help get them ready for the next steps after foster care. Some states are mandated to provide living skills for the youth in foster care.

Juvenile Detention Centers

Juvenile detention centers can be for sentenced youth up to age eighteen, where they stay for the duration of their sentences or commitments. Youths can also be detained at the centers on a short-term basis while awaiting trial, or while awaiting placement in a long-term care program. In contrast to adults, juveniles go through a separate court system: the juvenile court, which sentences or commits juveniles to a certain program or facility. Some services are provided to youth while in detention: schooling, vocational training, and/or HiSET. Girls are now making up a larger share of the juvenile justice population at every stage of the process. LGBTQ youth represent 5–7 percent of the nation's overall youth population, but they compose 13–15 percent of those currently in the juvenile justice system.[1]

Day Centers for Previously Court-Involved Youth

For youth who have been previously incarcerated, there are organizations (usually nonprofit organizations) that work to help stabilize and reintegrate youth into the community after they have come out of court-ordered detention and treatment facilities. The day centers operated by these organizations are not easy to find—by a Google search, for example—but if you are working directly with a juvenile detention center, their staff can connect you to contacts within these facilities.

Alternative Schools

Sometimes the educational, behavioral, or medical needs of youth cannot be adequately met in a traditional educational environment. The teaching of these populations must often be more individualized, and the classes need to be smaller. Alternative schools can be quite useful in this regard.

Alcohol and Drug Recovery High Schools

These are considered alternative schools because they are public schools where students can earn a high school diploma, while being supported in their recovery from alcohol or drug use. Teens may attend an alternative school for a number of reasons; they could be a young parent and their public school was unable to provide the necessary care as well as education; they could be in foster care and their education has been interrupted a number of times and they are getting back on track; or they could have significant mental health and behavioral issues, and a public school setting is unable to provide the necessary help to address those issues as well as providing education. Overall, alternative schools focus on youths in a holistic way. Education is essential, of course, but there are other aspects to teens that make them whole, and alternative schools can often address those needs.

Organizations That Work with Immigrant and Refugee Teens

Some cities will have agencies that work directly with these populations; these are sometimes called the Office for Refugees and Immigrants. On the state level, there are often organizations that work with immigrants and may be called the Immigrant and Refugee Advocacy Coalition. And then there are national organizations like United We Dream that work directly with immigrant youth.

Other Populations That May Need Youth Services

There are some large populations whose teen members may need library outreach services. A few of these are as follow.

LGBTQIA teens. The acronym LGBT doesn't encompass all that it should. LGBTQIA is more encompassing and stands for "lesbian, gay, bisexual, transgender, queer/questioning, intersex, asexual," and there are several other terms (such as non-binary and pansexual) in use as well.

Gender and sexual orientation are important aspects of a teen's identity. Understanding and expressing one's sexual orientation and gender is a typical development task that varies across children and teens. For example, some teens may be unsure of their sexual orientation, whereas others have been clear about it since childhood and have expressed it since a young age. Expressing and exploring gender identity and roles is also a part of normal development. Unfortunately, lesbian, gay, bisexual, and transgender youth experience various challenges because of how others respond to their sexual orientation or gender identity/expression. This is also true for teens who are questioning their sexual orientation or gender identity, or who may be perceived as LGBTQIA or gender-variant by others.

Think about this in terms of how staff will respond and treat these teens. Think about training for all staff in the library who may be working directly with these populations.

Young parents. There are hospitals that work with young parents, shelters that house young parents and their children, and schools that will work directly with young parents.

New and non-readers. These teens may be found in any of the populations already mentioned.

THE NUTS AND BOLTS OF YOUTH FACILITIES

Homeless Shelters

Youth homeless shelters are most often for youth and young adults who are 16 to 24 years of age. Shelters for families or mature adults can be funded by state or city governments, but shelters for teens are almost always run by nonprofits or by religiously affiliated organizations. A homeless shelter can be a space for teens to access emergency services (with a specific number of beds and a specific number of nights for access), or it can be a space that provides long-term services for up to two or more years. A shelter will close at a certain time in the morning and teens will need to vacate the space. Some shelters do offer drop-in services for teens during the day, however. Basic services like food, laundry, and Wi-Fi are often provided, and more specific services like counseling, HiSET, job/vocational training, and housing services may also be offered. Teens are processed when they are accessing longer-term shelter, but they need only check in and give their names when using drop-in services.

In these shelters, the services are often on one floor and the rooms for sleeping are on another floor. Emergency beds can all be in one room, or they can be in separate spaces. Some programs may offer longer-term housing for teens, and focus on things like job or school readiness, or they may just serve as housing while the teens are working. These working teens will also be preparing for paying rent, and so they will pay a percentage of what they earn from their jobs to the shelter (for their housing).

Libraries may provide books to shelters. Some shelters will have a small deposit collection of books that are rotated. Often, however, shelters will not have any sort on collection on the premises at all.

Group Homes

Some group homes are in homes or apartment buildings in neighborhoods. There are no signs; they look like residences. These facilities are for more normalized teens. They are in the community, and their teens may attend the public schools. Some group homes, however, may be in a larger facility, and the teens aren't able to come and go of their free will. These facilities are dealing with teens who have more significant behavioral and/or psychiatric issues. Often these facilities will also have a private or public school on the grounds. Some of their programs are to prepare teens to transition back to their families, or go on to independent living. Group homes give youth the opportunity to acclimate into their community, and thereby enable an organic and successful transition. Each teen will often have their own room, or share with another teen their age. Depending on the facility itself, there may not be doors on the bedrooms, to maintain the security of the teens. Group homes, and even the more residential facilities will focus on counseling services and offer a fairly robust mental health program.

Since most group homes are private or are run through a nonprofit organization, they often don't have libraries or library services. A few may work with libraries where deposit collections may be rotated, or have librarians come in and provide some library services and programs.

Independent Living Skills Programs

ILSP programs aren't mandatory, but they are highly encouraged. Teens are given incentives to participate, such as free transportation, along with dinner and lunch as well. The programs focus on next steps and independent living skills, so things like laundry, budgeting, finding a job, and school and career preparedness are the chief topics of instruction, coaching, and counseling.

Juvenile Detention Centers

If teens commit a crime, they are processed in the juvenile court system. Then there are different pathways they may take. Some youth may be released directly back into the community, to undergo community-based rehabilitative programs, while others who pose a greater threat to themselves or others may serve time in a supervised juvenile detention center. These facilities may be private or they may be state-run. The facilities are secure, and not anyone can just walk into one of them. If the facility is a secure building, teens will walk through one door while the next is being unlocked; there are never multiple doors opened at once. Teens will attend school while in juvenile detention. That space is separate from their living area.

All of the teens' movements are monitored, and there is very little free movement. The living spaces have windows in the doors so that staff can always observe the teens if necessary. The doors to their living spaces are locked when they are inside. The living space will usually have a bunk bed and a bureau; bathrooms are shared spaces. There are a few counties and state-run juvenile detention centers which have partnerships with county or city public libraries, and there are even some, like the Alameda County (CA) Library Juvenile Hall, that will host libraries on the premises. There are many public libraries across the country that provide library services and programs to juvenile detention centers. Among these are the New York Public Library, the Boston Public Library, Brooklyn Public Library, Charlotte Mecklenburg Public Library, Hennepin County Public Library, and the Johnson County Public Library, to name only a few.

Alternative Schools

An alternative school may be run by the city or by a regional school system, or it may be supported by other agencies. These schools are often for teens who have dropped out of high school, or are at risk of doing so. Alternative schools will usually provide counseling services for teens who require a more supportive environment than a traditional high school. The classes tend to be smaller than those in the regular public schools, and they will usually offer students more support with academics. The school schedule may also be geared toward supporting teens who have outside responsibilities, like jobs or children. Like most schools, not anyone can just enter an alternative school: you need to be buzzed in and have a reason for being there. Apart from this, most alternative schools resemble their regular counterparts, though there is usually a smaller number of students than in a regular school.

Other potential partners might be:

- Juvenile detention centers
- Day centers that serve teens who were previously incarcerated
- Drug and alcohol recovery schools.

FEDERAL AND OTHER PROGRAMS TO ASSIST YOUTH

Under federal law, every school district must provide schooling to homeless youth and must provide a liaison for those students. The McKinney-Vento Homeless Education Assistance Act begins: "each State educational agency shall ensure that each child of a homeless individual and each homeless youth has equal access to the same free, appropriate public education, including a public preschool education, as provided to other children and youths." The act also states that "homeless children and youths should have access to the education and other services that such children and youths need to ensure that such children and youths have an opportunity to meet the same challenging State student academic achievement standards to which all students are held."

The McKinney-Vento Act provides federal funding for homeless shelter programs. The program is mandated to collaborate with state agencies, as well as with community providers, to support homeless families and their students. This is a federal act, therefore all school districts must work to ensure that homeless youth are able to attend school. Most school districts have a dedicated staff person who works with those teens in the district who are facing homelessness. Connecting with these staffers can be difficult because they may have large caseloads, but finding them listed in school district directories is quite easy. They are often listed as "homeless students/teens liaison" or as "homeless education resource coordinator." Connecting with these people means working with your school district.

There are various other programs that work to serve the educational needs of disadvantaged youths. These are all potential partners.

- Migrant Education Program. All U.S. states have a coordinator who works with the schools in that state to provide education to the children of migrant laborers. The goal of the Migrant Education Program is to ensure that all migrant students reach challenging academic standards and graduate with a high school diploma (or complete a HiSET) which prepares them for responsible citizenship, further learning, and productive employment. This is a federally administered and funded program that serves the children of migratory agricultural workers and fishermen.
- The EDCO Collaborative has a long and diverse history. It began in 1969 as a private consortium of public schools, and has continued to the present as a public collaborative. EDCO's mission has been consistent throughout its history; it focuses on the power of inter-district and inter-agency collaboration to meet the needs of underserved and at-risk students and adults. EDCO only operates in Massachusetts, but there are similar programs elsewhere in the United States, such as the many Head Start programs.
- Foster youth. Every school district is required to have a liaison under the provisions of the Fostering Connections to Success and Increasing Adoptions Act of 2008. This liaison serves as the point of contact with child welfare agencies to ensure school stability for the youth in foster care.
- LGBTQIA. Nationwide organizations like GLSEN (Gay Lesbian & Straight Education Network), the GSA (Gay Straight Alliance), and the True Colors Fund have local chapters in several high schools across the country. Most large cities have locals or chapters of these national organizations that work directly with LGBTQIA youth.
- Refugees and Immigrant Youth. National organizations like the Office of Refugee Resettlement
- Young parents, pregnant and parenting teens. There may be young parent programs in hospitals, the YMCA, school systems, and through state agencies like Child and Family Services.

FOLLOWING FACILITY POLICIES

Any outside organization with whom the library collaborates will be a "partner," but inside that partner's facilities, the library is a guest, and the partner is the host. You want to have good relations with your partner organizations. The organizations you work with will have their own rules, regulations, and policies. The library needs to be aware of what those rules are, and they may also need to be included in the MOU, so that all library staff working with the organization know the responsibilities of each partner, as well as the partner's policies. For example, in some juvenile detention facilities, there are dress codes for staff and for visitors. The staff may not be allowed to talk about anything personal with teens, and visitors are expected to do the same. There may also be books with specific content that cannot be allowed in a facility.

It may be our librarians' natural tendency to want to provide access to books and not censor them, but the reality is that there are valid security and management reasons why some organizations don't allow certain types of content in their facilities. Librarians, as guests, need to honor these regulations when partnering with these entities. These are conversations to have with potential partner organizations before beginning any partnership. Safety is a concern in many facilities, and you need to know what the procedures are for any situation that could be deemed unsafe. The partner organizations are responsible for ensuring the safety of their teens, and they are also responsible for the content of the material that is shared with teens. These organizations need to make you aware of and to follow their policies. Keep their policies, rules, and concerns in mind when you're making a training manual for partnerships.

Here are some things to ask the facility beforehand and even make part of a handbook:

1. Is there any training for library staff to participate in, to get a sense of the partner's policies and procedures?
2. Are there any policies that the facility expects the library to follow, and if so, what are they?
3. Is there a dress code when inside the facility?
4. If the library is bringing books into the facility, library staff will need to know what content is not allowed in the facility. Think about some sort of system where you could perhaps share the book titles with links, so that facility staff can get a sense of the book titles before they come into the facility.
5. Will library staff be escorted by facility staff, or will they have free rein?
6. Is there anything that library staff can or cannot bring into the facility, like cell phones or writing materials, and if so, what are they?
7. If a teen says something inappropriate to library staff, what is the reporting procedure?

Library Programs and Services in the Partner's Facility

What will your library be providing in terms of library services and/or programming in the facility? Often with outreach services, only one or two librarians may be participating in outreach visits, so whatever you're providing must be easily transportable. If your services will consist of books, think about how you will transport them around, because as you know, books can get heavy. If you are working with a juvenile detention center, there may be rules as to the content of materials that can be brought in. Think about creating an MOU with facilities like this, to help avoid any potential issues before they happen. If the facility hasn't worked with your library before, sharing with them exactly what you have in mind for your program will be helpful, and can be tweaked if needed.

Going into a facility may require library staff to be CORI-cleared (Criminal Offender Record Information) or fingerprinted. Again, this is something that needs to be discussed before going in. Issues with materials, or with facility staff, should be discussed with both partners. This conversation should be between partners only, and not in front of facility youth. If this type of miscommunication might occur, be sure to work it out before the first library visit. It's always good to solicit feedback from facility staff, and even more importantly, from the teens. Your role in the partnership includes gathering information and feedback from the participants (the teens) about how the program is working.

You may also find yourself working with several different staff members in different types of facilities. These staffers can include:

- Law officers, social workers, teachers (juvenile detention facilities)
- Social workers, case workers, youth workers, teachers (homeless shelters)
- Social workers, psychiatrists, case workers, youth workers, teachers, group home caregivers, Department of Children and Family caseworkers/social workers (group homes and foster homes)
- Teachers, teacher assistants, psychiatrists, social workers, drug and alcohol case managers (alternative schools)
- Refugee and immigrant youth workers, case workers, social workers, youth workers, teachers

SOME TEENS YOU MIGHT WORK WITH

To what teen demographic will you be providing outreach? The list below is just a sampling of some of the teens you might encounter in your outreach efforts. This list is not exhaustive, and is given merely to provide examples and context.

- A teen who ran away from home and has been living on the streets for over a year. He is trying to find a job, but is also struggling with addiction.
- A teen who is incarcerated.
- A teen attending an alternative school. She has a two-year old daughter, lives at home with her mother, and has a 30-hour a week job.
- A teen who is attending an alternative school, who is challenged by living in a foster home, has no contact with her family, and has oppositional defiant disorder (a childhood disorder marked by a pattern of hostile, disobedient, and defiant behaviors directed at adults or other authority figures. Children with the disorder also display angry and irritable moods, as well as argumentative and vindictive behavior.)
- A teen who left his native country due to war and has been living with several family members (who are not his parents). None of the family speaks English, so they rely on this teen for translating.
- A trans teen living in a group home whose family disowned him due to his trans status.
- A teen who was incarcerated for over a year and is now back in the community.

You must meet teens where they are at the moment. You don't need to ask questions about why they are where they are, or what they did. This by no means excludes giving them your compassion, but it does mean treating everyone the same.

FORMING A LASTING PARTNERSHIP

You want your partnerships to be sustainable and successful. Part of this depends on evaluating the impact of the outreach services you provide (see chapter 4). The other part is building open communication with your partner(s).

- You should identify goals and outcomes with the partner organization and share them regularly, maybe annually via a report. The report should also include statistics and maybe even anecdotes from the teens themselves. If you formed an MOU with your partner, you may have identified year-end check-ins on the progress, successes, failures, and challenges of your outreach service. These kinds of continuing conversations are helpful in determining if things need to be changed or modified. If you don't have an MOU, it is extremely important to maintain open communication with your partners.

- You should identify both partners' expectations initially, before you start outreach. Clear expectations are helpful for both organizations.
- MOUs are a helpful tool to identify the responsibilities for each organization in a partnership. If things aren't working with your partner organization, the MOU can be something to refer to, and then determine if the partnership will continue.
- Talk often and be clear. If you and your partner organization(s) have year-end evaluations, that's great, but if there are questions or issues that come up before the year's end, talk about them immediately.
- It's okay if the partnership doesn't work out; it's better to find that out earlier than later. Be sure to communicate amicably at the end of a partnership.

EXAMPLE A: PARTNERING WITH COMMUNITY ORGANIZATIONS

Jennifer Bisson is the teen services librarian at the Greenwood Branch of the Seattle Public Library. She has been a youth services librarian for seventeen years, and has worked at the Greenwood Branch for seven years.

What does the outreach look like?

"I work with two local Boys and Girls Clubs during the summer to host teen programs specifically for them. This year we are hosting programs for teens in grades six through eight, like a sound design workshop, creating a web app, and bucket drumming," Jennifer says. "The focus of Boys and Girls Clubs is this: to help young people, especially those whose needs are great, to build strong character and realize their full potential as responsible citizens and leaders. We do this by providing a safe haven filled with hope and opportunity, cultivating ongoing relationships with caring adults, and offering life-enhancing programs."

Jennifer also hosts a program for teen volunteers to earn their service learning requirements through their schools. The volunteers meet at the Boys and Girls Club once a week, and provide literacy support and logic/math skills game-playing to second and third graders. This is one-on-one support and mentoring. The teens are trained and supported throughout the whole session, which lasts for 10–12 weeks. There are two sessions per school year. This program, called Learning Buddies, is great for the second- and third-grade children participating, but it is also a job training/preparatory program for the teens and a way for them to earn their service learning hours. This program is the only one done off-site because Jennifer wants to reach the target population who are in the Boys and Girls Club after school. The teens come from area public and private high schools. Among the last batch of eighteen teen volunteers, about one-third of them spoke one or more languages besides English.

The Seattle Public Library partners with a local writing center called the Bureau of Fearless Ideas (BFI). The library hosts a teen tutoring program twice a week at its facilities during the school year. Jennifer says, "This is a highly successful program serving 90 percent first-generation immigrant, college-bound teens. The BFI didn't have the funding to continue to keep their building open four nights a week, so twice a week the program is offered at the library. The BFI recruits and trains all their own volunteer tutors. The library works with this organization in other capacities with children, but this is another way in which we serve teens."

While the Seattle Public Library identifies several organizations and populations that it provides outreach to, the Greenwood Branch focuses on the two area Boys and Girls Clubs and the BFI program. The library pulls teen volunteers from three area public high schools and four area private high schools. MOUs have been created to outline the responsibilities of each organization so everyone knows what they are responsible for.

How do things work when the library's programs/ services are delivered at an outside facility?

With the BFI, it is an "outreach-inreach" arrangement because they need the library's space to house the program, while the library needs the BFI to bring the teens and the tutors to its space. This partnership may not seem like "outreach," but it was born from several years of partnerships and good relations with the BFI as a community partner. Jennifer says, "All of the outreach has allowed teens to think of the library as a place to help and support their program. As for Learning Buddies at the Boys and Girls Club, the library brings along the teens it has recruited, trained, and supported, the club provides the kids and the space, and the library provides a staff member during the sessions."

The summer teen programs are paid for by the library and can be hosted at either location. The library also vets the performers and educators, as well as finding quality STEM programming that community partners may not be able to afford or locate. Sometimes the library is the better host because it has air conditioning, a projector, laptop computers, and so on. In many ways, the library is a more desirable space, so the teen camps like to come there.

EXAMPLE B: PARTNERING WITH COMMUNITY ORGANIZATIONS

Kate McNair is the teen services coordinating librarian at the Johnson County Library in Kansas. She has been a teen librarian providing outreach services for more than twelve years.

What does outreach look like at the Johnson County Library?

The Johnson County Library provides outreach services to children, teens, and adults who might not otherwise have access to library services. One population they have served for over fifteen years is the teens in the Juvenile Detention Center. The outreach is a service provided by both the Youth Services and Information Services departments. The library has also found that outreach to justice-involved populations requires consistency and dedication. There is a committee of nine staff members who provide services and programs to teens and adults in corrections facilities and court services programs. Service to underserved populations has been part of the library's strategic plan goals for decades. Serving justice-involved people has been part of the library's work for over fifteen years, and in that time they have grown the program from two library staffers to nine and from two library branches to seven.

The library serves justice-involved teens in three facilities/programs. Among these, the Johnson County Juvenile Detention Center holds teens awaiting detention hearings, state custody placement, placement into a juvenile correctional facility, or release back to a parent/guardian. The facility's population is largely male, and the average length of stay there is about two weeks. Many aspects of this facility would look familiar to someone imagining a stereotypical jail on *Law and Order*. The walls are beige, all doors are locked, and there are cameras all through the building. The teens (who are called "clients") wear beige jumpsuits and live in pods with six to ten other teens. In the eleven years Kate has been providing services to this building, she has seen its average daily population drop from 80 teens to less than 20, in large part thanks to juvenile justice reform initiatives at the state level.

What do the library's services look like?

The Johnson County Library is fortunate to have received grants that helped build libraries in two of the program facilities. In each building, these collections have their own dedicated space. Each collection holds 700–800 items which have been purchased specifically for it (i.e., they are not part of the library's public collection). These collections are maintained and updated by library staff in consultation with corrections staff and teen residents. To help encourage the teens' familiarity with how the public library works, each book spine is labeled with the same classification as those in the public library.

To check out items, teens don't need a library card, and they don't even have to "check them out." They need only take a book off the shelf and enjoy it. Corrections staff help by returning books to the library and reshelving them (sometimes with the help of teen resident volunteers).

What do these programs look like?

Our philosophy is to bring the library services you would find inside the public library to buildings where teens may not have access to the same opportunities. Accordingly, some of the units have hosted book clubs, discussion groups, and author visits. The bimonthly program called Library ETC (Explore, Tinker, Connect) uses library resources to teach 21st-century skills like collaboration, critical thinking, creativity, and problem-solving. The program includes interactive booktalks, writing workshops (facilitated by library staff and local authors), art workshops (generally using outside facilitators), and 3D modeling and printing.

With regard to technology programming, the Corrections staff are reluctant to allow cameras or devices with Wi-Fi access into the facility. This means that when laptops are brought in to the facility, the staff must lock down the camera and Wi-Fi so they can only be used with administrator access. The staff must also wipe all identifying data from the laptops after the program (for instance, if a teen saves a file with their name, the staff might need to anonymize it).

For the 3D Mashup and Fidget Spinner programs, Kate must pre-select the templates for teens to use. They cannot use web-based programs like Tinkercad, so instead they use offline tools like SketchUp (which is not ideal for the program). But Kate has found that almost any library program can be modified for these facilities.

The following is an example of a popular 3D mashup program.

PROGRAM OVERVIEW

In this fifty-minute program, participants will use SketchUp (a 3D modeling computer program) to make a 3D model that mashes up two template models. Participants will learn about 3D printing process and resources. Participants will be expected to:

- Think about creative ways to mash up their scan
- Help each other problem-solve how to turn their vision into reality
- Deal with the frustration of learning a new tool or piece of software

Final Product: A customized 3D mashup that can be used as a game piece or just for fun.

The Johnson County Library is very fortunate to have a robust makerspace at its Central Resource Library. There are several 3D printers and laptops available there for outreach and programs. Prior to teens' arrival at the library, the staff will have checked out the printers, loaded them with fresh filament, and double-checked to make sure that everything is working. They will also secure the laptops to lock down all cameras and Wi-Fi access (these are requirements from the Corrections partners, and the staff have done this long enough so that they have a profile on each laptop, which makes the process easier).

Setup

Before teens arrive in the room, Kate sets up the 3D printer with a sample print, so they can see it in action. Kate sets out all the laptops (which are closed, since they are just too much temptation when open) and a mouse (this really seems to help, since trackpads can be tricky if you aren't used to them).

Welcome

As the teens file in, they grab a desk and a laptop (the setup can accommodate up to ten participants, and if there are more, they can pair up and work together). We start with introductions, and the teens are asked for their first names and their familiarity with a 3D printer. ("Never heard of it, I have heard of one, I have seen one, I have used one.")

Before we even start with the models, the teens look at the 3D printer, which is hopefully about halfway through its sample print. They talk about what they notice, how they think it works, and what it reminds them of. Kate tells them a little about the printing process (PLA plastic, how much a printer costs, etc.) and points out the services available in the makerspace. She passes around sample prints (complete and incomplete) so the teens can see how they will feel and look (and they also look at the inside of the 3D print sample).

3D Printing

When the teens sit back down at their laptops, Kate goes over the goals for the day (mashing up two 3D models), and the teens play around with the 3D modeling software (they use SketchUp, but if you are doing this in a place with internet access, Tinkercad is *much* more user-friendly). Once everyone has learned the necessary scaling, rotating, and moving skills, they then start in on the task at hand.

Kate gives a handout with directions and walks the teens through the tutorial, but she's not concerned if they want to race ahead and do things on their own. Everyone has their own learning pace, and she would rather they follow their inner compass than try to hold the group to one trajectory.

Reflection

At the end of the fifty minutes, the teens take a moment to talk about what they liked and what they found frustrating (and how they dealt with that frustration). Kate says this feedback is great because it helps to improve the workshop for the next group, and it is also a great opportunity for the teens to reflect on how they overcame a setback, or dealt with anger after a perceived failure. "I take time to compliment those who struggled, those who helped others, and those who were engaged the whole time—both to the teens themselves and to the Corrections staff members in the room, who can add positive feedback to their records," says Kate.

WORKING WITH OUTSIDE PARTNERS

Working with outside partners in providing outreach isn't something that just happens overnight. It takes time, energy, consistency, and communication. Because the outside partners are just that, outside the library, remember to be clear and concise about what you are going to provide, when, and how. They are not internal partners, so you don't directly supervise them. And there is nothing that makes them beholden to the library except the success of the outreach. You should have a good understanding about the populations you will be working with. And you should understand that consistency is something that has been missing from most of these teens' lives, so try and make the library something that is consistent and safe.

NOTE

1. Youth First Initiative, "50,000 Children: The Geography of America's Dysfunctional & Racially Disparate Youth Incarceration Complex," www.youthfirstinitiative.org/thefacts/.

3

The Role of Staff in Providing Outreach

Now that you have some notion of how to create partnerships, you may want to think about who in your library will be providing the outreach. Is it important that a credentialed teen librarian provide the outreach? Of course, teen services librarians should be involved, whether in developing the partnership or in developing the outreach plan itself. The actual implementation of the outreach service or program can be done by library assistants and paraprofessionals, but there does need to be organizational and coordinating involvement from a teen librarian.

If the staff possesses the following characteristics, they will go a long way in working with teens. What are the characteristics of an effective teen librarian or assistant? According to YALSA, this librarian must:

- Be creative and enthusiastic in working with teens.
- Have strong and flexible problem-solving skills.
- Have an excellent customer service ethic.
- Be passionate about helping teens gain the skills they need to be successful in their personal and academic pursuits.
- Be passionate about providing outreach services to underserved and underrepresented teens.

- Be aware of the challenges that teens in custody, in foster care, or in transition face.
- Be empathetic while working with teens who are facing challenging life situations.
- Be an effective communicator with teens from diverse backgrounds.
- Be flexible and be able to accommodate unpredictable schedules and unexpected changes.
- Be consistent and reliable.
- Be open to collaboration and compromise.

WRITING YOUR JOB DESCRIPTION

Your job description as a teen librarian may already exist, and what you're doing may not accurately reflect those focus areas. Even in the last ten years there have been new focus areas within teen services, like outreach, and you may be doing things that aren't reflected in the job description. They should be. If outreach is something you are doing and is an important aspect of your job, it should be in the job description. If creating and maintaining partnerships with organizations that serve underrepresented teens is part of your job, that too should be in the job description. You should write out the target areas you want to hone in on; creating and maintaining partnerships, and providing outreach. Share this document with your supervisor, and then discuss with her whether those areas should be part of your job description. Moreover, if the description is rewritten, it will be a more comprehensive representation of your duties, and so it will keep that job position relevant well into the future.

The section below is a generic job description for a teen librarian. Outreach is listed as a focus in the first line. Based on all the responsibilities, outreach comprises roughly 25 percent of the tasks overall. In a 40-hour workweek, this would mean that 10 hours of that week would be devoted to performing outreach services. Does your job description include outreach? The job description is an excellent tool to accurately describe your responsibilities, and as a measure of those responsibilities it can help with your performance evaluations, and can also be used to advocate for responsibilities you may not be focusing on.

Teen Librarian Job Description

1. Assists in the development, planning, and implementation of the library's program of service to teens through reference and readers' advisory services, outreach, and in-house programs.

2. Participates in the development of interactive relationships within a defined neighborhood and in the implementation of activities to stimulate community use of the library's resources, *especially through schools*, and through other agencies which serve teens.
3. Plans and conducts comprehensive programming for teens.
4. Performs readers' advisory services and difficult or involved reference service for the public.
5. Provides instruction to increase patrons' skills in the use of book resources and electronic databases.
6. Manages the funds assigned to teen services.
7. Participates in the development of the teen book collection and manages the appropriate materials budget.
8. Assists in the compilation of annotated lists and bibliographies involving book and non-book materials, especially for teens.
9. Is responsible for presentations and written reports on teen activities within the branch library.
10. May be responsible for day-to-day operations of the branch in the absence of the Branch Librarian or other ranking staff member.
11. May participate in recommending and/or planning changes in services or new services for teens.
12. Actively participates in system-wide committees, training, and other professional activities.
13. Performs other related and/or comparable duties as assigned.

Updating Your Performance Evaluation

Your areas of focus, goals, and objectives should be reflected in your job description. If you are performing outreach, this should be reflected in the job description, but it should also be part of your performance evaluation. Who are you working with? Have you established new partnerships, or new programs or services with your outreach partners? Your supervisor should be aware of all of this. Goals should be established with each of the partners you are working with and each of the outreach services you are providing.

CREATING AN INTERNSHIP PROGRAM IN OUTREACH SERVICES

In 2019, I created a formal internship program in Teen Central of the Boston Public Library, and we partnered with Simmons University to offer a for-credit internship to MLIS students. The internship focuses on observation, as well as on researching and responding to real-life situations in libraries that one doesn't learn in library school, via conversations with librarians and on the internet. In the course of the program, the interns are exposed to the outreach partnerships our library has created, and what those services look like.

Goals and Vision of the Internship Program

Vision. The internship experience will expose the interns to numerous facets of the public library, but with a specific focus on teen services and outreach services to teens.

Goal 1. The interns will gain an essential knowledge of the structure of a public library as an institution.

Goal 2. The interns will gain an essential knowledge of teen services, programming, and outreach services.

Goal 3. The interns will gain more confidence in a professional library setting.

Potential Benefits for the Library

- The opportunity to train and invest in the next generation of librarians (including identifying potential future employees)
- Access to new perspectives, ideas, and skill sets
- Support in providing professional development opportunities for existing staff (for example, developing management skills)
- The opportunity for self-reflection and evaluation, facilitated by sharing staff members' expertise with interns
- Opportunities to build and sustain partnerships with educational institutions and communities
- Furthering the library's mission of reaching out to and providing educational opportunities to the community

Potential Benefits for the Interns

- Opportunities for high-quality, hands-on experience in a real-world library setting, including mentorship, job-shadowing, and exposure to different kinds of library roles and projects
- Professional skills development and resume-building in a supportive environment
- Building new professional relationships, networks, job contacts, and potential references
- Opportunities to gain and fulfill academic credits and requirements, all while applying real-world practice to academic learning

Sample Curriculum

- Read the mission of the library.
- Read the library's collection development policy.
- Become familiar with the library's quarterly usage reports.
- Become familiar with the library's policies and procedures.
- Read the article "How Essential Are Library Spaces for Teens?" in *Voice of Youth Advocates*, Bernier, June 2019, online.
- Find an article in *School Library Journal*, the YALSA Blog, or the *Journal of Research on Libraries and Young Adults*, and share why it was important to you.
- Read the article "Library Outreach to Teens" in *Young Adult Library Services*, Snow, 2009, volume 8, number 1.
- Read the article "Library Services to Teens in Foster Care" in *Voice of Youth Advocates*, Snow, 2019, online.
- Read the YALSA Blog posts on "Outreach Services for Teen Library Staff: What Some Staff are Doing outside the Walls of Libraries," YALSA Blog, online.
- Create interview questions, and interview the teen librarians throughout the system.
- Read Jennifer Velasquez's article Young Adult Outreach: An Examination of Outreach Attempts at Branch Libraries in a Large Urban Public Library System, *Journal of Library Administration,* 2019, volume 59, number 2.
- Make twice-monthly visits to alternative schools.
- Make a monthly visit to the Department of Youth Services.
- Read the chapter "A Vision for an Innovative Teen Space" by Snow, Dowds, and Halpin, in the book *Create, Innovate, and Serve: A Radical Approach to Children's and Youth Programming*, edited by Campana and Mills, 2019
- Find two job descriptions for a teen librarian or outreach services librarian that you find comprehensive and interesting.
- Identify questions you might ask a hiring committee in a job interview based on the job descriptions.
- Participate in a mock job interview with a committee.
- Meet with the other interns for thirty minutes each week in order to check in with them.
- Put together a research of the experiences as well as responding to specific questions.

THE LACK OF DIVERSITY AMONG LIBRARIANS

As a teen librarian, you may well be working with populations that are under-served, and most of those populations do not reflect the demographics of our profession. About 86 percent of librarians are white, and 82 percent of librarians are female.[1] The librarian profession suffers from a lack of diversity and shows no signs of changing anytime soon. Does this mean that white librarians shouldn't perform outreach or work with teens of color? It doesn't, but what the data points out is the reality of our profession, and our profession's disparity with the populations we serve. White privilege, as both a legacy and a cause of racism, is something that Peggy McIntosh pointed out in her essay "White Privilege: Unpacking the Invisible Knapsack," and this is something of which we should all be aware. The idea of providing outreach services to underserved teens shouldn't be looked at through the lens of a White Savior, or with the library being a savior, but there does need to be some acknowl-edgment by white librarians of the need for improved cultural competence on their part. The YALSA report *The Future of Library Services for and with Teens: A Call to Action* points out significant shifts in the demographics of teens, and how cultural competence recognizes the significance of culture in our own lives and the lives of others. The report advocates that we come to know and respect diversity through our interactions with individuals from diverse lin-guistic, cultural, and socioeconomic groups; and that we fully integrate the culture of diverse groups into our services, work, and institutions in order to enhance the lives of both those being served by the library profession and those engaged in service.[2]

EXAMPLE A: REACHING OUT INTO THE COMMUNITY

Pamela McCarter is the equity initiative leader/outreach coordinator for the Char-lotte Mecklenburg (NC) Library.

Pamela states, "I like to say my career in outreach began when I was in fourth grade. There was no physical library in my small community, and I had an abundance of great books that I received from the school librarian each sum-mer. I set up a self-checkout system and allowed children in the neighborhood to check out these books. I only charged fines if the book was lost or dam-aged. I also lent my reading services to a neighbor with deteriorating vision. That began my love of providing resources and materials to those who were underserved.

"In an official capacity, I have been in the Outreach Department for 10 years and have been with the Charlotte Mecklenburg Library for 23 years serving children, teens, and adults.

"I believe that beyond being people-focused and passionate, there are a few additional characteristics that are important in providing outreach: assertiveness, being strategic, confident, inclusive, compassionate, adaptable, a multidimensional thinker, collaborative, innovative, relatable, communicative, good listener, and community-driven. We provide access to communities that are often underrepresented and/or minoritized. There is a staff person to advocate for making a difference in the community. One of my favorite programs over the years was collaboration with the Boy Scouts. This outreach work with one Boy Scout troop led to me being able to take several teens on the Boys Scouts' annual ski trip. That exposure made a difference in the lives of many of the youth who joined me over the four years of the partnership.

"The Charlotte Mecklenburg Library provides staff access, materials, and resources to all members of Mecklenburg County, our nontraditional customers are included. That's why outreach is important. We try to duplicate any program that happens in-house at an outreach location. Much of my time is split working with teens and adults in the custody of the Mecklenburg County Sheriff Department, the reentry population (people who were previously incarcerated, and may be on probation or on parole), and older adults in adult day programs.

"The Outreach Services Department's goals are to provide services to high-need and underserved populations. Throughout the year, the department takes to the community—at low-performing schools, senior living centers, correctional facilities, recreation centers, hospitals, centers for individuals living with disabilities, refugee centers, laundromats, and more—to lead informative and engaging programs like storytimes, computer and technology classes, writing workshops, parent literacy workshops, job readiness activities, sensory programs (programs for people with sensory-processing issues), book discussions, and library resources overviews.

"The entire department of seven outreach coordinators and one manager provides outreach programs and services. Most days we work independently of each other, but on occasions we look for opportunities to collaborate. Outreach is for everyone. No one job title is responsible for outreach and no position is excluded, if they desire. We have everyone from library assistants to branch managers providing outreach. Mecklenburg County spans 567 square miles, and it takes everyone to provide equitable service. Each branch is responsible for providing outreach in their community and adding it to their fiscal programming plan.

"Annually, an outreach training retreat is hosted for all staff who are interested in outreach programming. Whether they are new to the organization or just need a refresher, they will explore a variety of topics to help them perform their outreach with confidence. The full-day retreat is organized by the Outreach Advisory Team. This team is made up of a variety of library staff and Outreach Department members. The day is filled with resources and tools, ranging from outreach guidelines to how to find your community's demographics, to writing stories of impact. The Outreach Department also provides mentoring and coaching for branches and individuals. Staff can participate in our shadowing/feedback opportunity, for additional support.

"I see a very diverse group of staff providing outreach in our organization. From the Outreach Department to staff providing outreach in the branches, the diversity is great. It closely mirrors the makeup of the community. We have a diverse group of all ages, races, ethnicity, sex, years of service, and positions."

EXAMPLE B: REACHING OUT INTO THE COMMUNITY

Sharon McKellar is the supervising librarian for teen services at the Oakland Public Library.

"Outreach has been a part of library services at the Oakland Public Library (OPL) since at least 2003. I have been providing outreach services there to some extent for fifteen years. The Teen Services Department was formed right around the time I began at OPL, and so we have been providing outreach to teens formally for at least that long, but I know that services to teens were provided by a committee even before that time.

"The Oakland Public Library provides a variety of outreach services by different staff members in different roles throughout the system. Currently the Teen Services Department has a teen outreach librarian position, and the Children's Services Department has two outreach librarians. These three librarians help coordinate outreach to their respective age groups systemwide. In addition, the staff at each branch are doing local outreach to all age groups. The teen librarians and our 'teen partners' (library staff who are committed to working with teens at locations without a teen librarian) throughout the library system are responsible for doing outreach to teens in their communities, and have a lot of freedom in what that outreach might look like. The outreach librarian also coordinates outreach materials, ensuring that Teen Services has plenty of relevant, up-to-date information which can be brought to any outreach opportunity, in schools or otherwise.

"Among the materials that we may provide at the point of outreach are resource guides which point young people to local and online resources on a wide variety of topics, including mental health, sex and sexuality, homework assistance, finding a job, and financial aid and scholarships. With these we hope to demonstrate the library as a judgment-free source of relevant information on things that teens care about, including those topics that teens may feel less comfortable approaching staff about.

"The library formed an outreach team which has been active for a few years now. This team is made up of the three previously mentioned librarians, adult services librarians focused on outreach, and library assistants who assist with outreach as a main component of their job. We also call on a multitude of other staff members to attend off-site events and assist with outreach.

"We do a lot of work with schools—both students and teachers—with community organizations by attending and tabling at local events, and with churches and other neighborhood gathering places. In Teen Services, we also work to ensure we are doing outreach to underserved populations, including justice-impacted young people.

"In partnership with the local school district, we have been piloting a project to provide every student with a full-service library card on the back of their student ID. This has created a large and systematic opportunity for OPL's Teen Services to outreach to middle and high school teachers on their formal professional development days, where we can share all of the resources we can offer their students. With this work, every student in a school has a library card and every teacher understands the resources offered by the library, even without setting foot in a physical library building. This has the potential for huge impact, especially in communities and schools that don't have access to a lot of resources otherwise, including those without school libraries or librarians.

"We offer many services and resources to young people who are exiting the juvenile justice system, and we want to make sure they're aware that we're here and happy to support them. We are very lucky to have a talented library assistant on staff as part of Teen Services who has been doing volunteer work in Juvenile Hall in Alameda County, and who has worked for many years with teens impacted by the juvenile justice system. This member of our staff has been able to use her connections in the Juvenile Hall and in the community to pilot a Juvie to Library pipeline program. With this program, we hope that young people leaving the Hall will see the library as a safe and friendly space and as a resource for them.

"We believe strongly in letting staff at all levels bring their passions to work, and we know that we are a better library system doing better work and more successful outreach when this isn't being done exclusively by librarians. The work we do in Juvenile Hall is one great example of this.

"That same staff member also runs the Oakland Public Library's Youth Poet Laureate Program and is able to bring library-sponsored writing work-shops to Juvenile Hall, to support incarcerated young people in completing their applications to the Youth Poet Laureate program. This has been impactful and successful. The young people who are part of our Youth Poet Laureate pro-gram can then speak their truth to audiences of all ages and all types through-out Oakland and the Bay Area, and they often bring writing workshops into the schools. These youth leaders help us spread the word about their work and our work, creating more awareness of library programs among other young people. It's an amazing and positive cycle of outreach.

"All of this also helps create a more diverse team of people providing outreach to the community. When we're not relying entirely on librarian staff, we are able to reach our communities far more effectively. We can ensure outreach to places with large Spanish- or Arabic-speaking populations by having Spanish- or Arabic-speaking staff members present, for example.

"In addition to diversity in staff, we aim for diversity in the services that we can provide while doing outreach. The Oakland Public Library has a fleet of three library bikes that are available to attend outreach events, and a team of staff members who can ride them. These vehicles are nimble, easy to use, and allow for great flexibility in our outreach. We also have collections of giveaway books, called our 'Share the Love' collection, which we bring to outreach events. They are stickered with a 'Read it. Love it. Pass it on' OPL-branded sticker and are given away without any checking-out required. We also have a zine collection that we bring to outreach events. Zines provide a great opportunity to reach underserved and marginalized populations by providing hyper-local resources, and resources that might not ever be published by a traditional publisher.

"With our large team of staff members providing outreach, a smaller group of specialized staff providing coordination of outreach, and a variety of flexible materials available for outreach, our staff is empowered to reach into our community as broadly and deeply as possible, providing resources, materials, and opportunities to teens throughout Oakland."

THE LIBRARY PROFESSION

We know that our profession is overwhelmingly white, and some of the populations of teens we will be working with are not white. This is just a reminder to heighten our awareness, and not an apology on the part of the librarian. It is important to be cognizant of prejudices and barriers that face teens of color, as well as every single population we are talking about in this book. This doesn't necessarily mean that outreach should be provided by librarians of color or by the populations of which we speak, but it does mean that all librarians should try to be culturally aware and competent.

Some libraries, due to union parameters, will only allow credentialed librarians to provide outreach and not library assistants. You should work within the parameters of your individual library.

NOTES

1. Data USA, "Librarians," https://datausa.io/profile/soc/254021/.
2. Young Adult Library Services Association, *The Future of Library Services for and with Teens: A Call to Action*, www.ala.org/yaforum/sites/ala.org.yaforum/files/content/YALSA_nationalforum_final.pdf.

4

How to Identify Goals and Outcomes for Outreach Services

The goal is the desired outcome(s) of your service or program, and the objectives are the different strategies you use to achieve the goal.

It is important to identify goals and objectives for your outreach efforts, to determine whether you are succeeding in those efforts. And how can you be sure you were successful in achieving what you set out to do initially? By using statistics and other measures to track the outcomes of your services and programs, and thereby measure their success.

Goals should be specific, measurable, achievable, and timely. They should be revisited each year, with the possibility of updating or changing them and the objectives. You should think about sharing these goals with your outreach partners as well. Goal-setting may also help if you are considering grant-writing for your outreach or fundraising. You should always keep track of the number of teens you see on your outreach visits, the number of programs that teens participate in, and the number of books and/or requests that you handle.

When creating goals, think about setting them for each of your outreach partners:

- What do you want the program or service to accomplish?
- Are there skills or competencies you want the teens to acquire or improve upon?
- Do you want to increase the number of teens you are serving with your partner? Do you want to expand your library's outreach to include more partnerships?

EXAMPLES OF GOALS

Goal 1: The library will provide twelve unique technology programs annually to teens who are homeless. (programs in a homeless shelter)
　　The strategy: What actions will you take to meet this goal?

- Identify one partner to provide six of these programs.
- The Teen Librarian will provide the other six of these programs.
- Half of the curriculum for this technology programming will be based on successful programs that teens in the teen space have already participated in. The other half of the curriculum will be developed six months before the implementation of the programs.

Goal 2: Teens will learn one new skill through participation in these technology programs.
　　The strategy: What actions will you take to meet this goal?

- Identify three skills that teens can learn by participating in a program.
- Survey each teen before participation in said program to determine what they know and don't know.
- Survey each teen after participation to determine if they learned any new skills.

Goal 3: The library will increase the number of book requests from teens by 10 percent and fill those requests.
　　The strategy: What actions will you take to meet this goal?

- The library will order more books, and Teen Services will benefit from this by being able to fill more teen requests.
- With the grant the library received, Teen Services will have the ability to create, or expand, a core collection of books to fill more requests from teens in the homeless shelter the library is working with.

EVALUATING THE IMPACT OF OUTREACH SERVICES

Setting and keeping track of your goals is important; these goals are not just something you look at once a year. At the end of the year, you assess whether you met the goals and decide whether to continue the program or services, make changes to them, or discontinue them altogether.

If your library doesn't have an outreach services department, what is the benefit of having a goal, a strategy, and tracking outcomes and statistics? You can connect all of these to your library's mission and strategic plan, and then share your data with the library's administration. You'll need to show the need for outreach services, as well as the potential for using that information to apply for grants or other types of funding.

USING GOALS TO CONTINUALLY IMPROVE OUTREACH SERVICES

Goals are something that you visit again and again. Each year you will analyze those goals and outcomes to be sure they were met, and determine if any changes and updates need to be made to the goals. You can gather data in various ways. Keeping track of numbers is always good, since this can demonstrate a higher usage of materials by teens. You can also gather anecdotal feedback from the teens who participate in your programs or services. You may want to have teens participate in surveys before and after a specific program or service, in order to help you determine whether it was successful or not.

Here's an example: a library is partnering with a safety net hospital. (A safety net hospital is a type of medical center that by legal obligation or mission provides health care to individuals regardless of their insurance status or ability to pay. This legal mandate forces safety net hospitals to serve all populations.) A librarian makes a monthly visit to the adolescent ward of the hospital, with a total of fifty books to distribute. The visit takes a total of eight hours of prep time; this includes the time spent retrieving books, writing up booktalks, checking out books, and transporting them to the hospital each month. There are an average of twelve teens who participate in the program each month. While these numbers are low, the teens that do participate have no access to books in the hospital otherwise, and they may be in the hospital for the long term.

You should obtain input from the librarian regularly about the value and success of the program. Is the program sustainable and worth keeping? Yes, with some tweaks and changes. Go back to the goals and outcomes for the program, and don't forget to look at the input from the teens. The total amount of time for the monthly visit may need to change, to adequately reflect the number of teens participating, and so the number of hours the librarian is putting into the prep time and the outreach visit will have to be adjusted. This update to the program will allow for more outreach by the librarian, a change that is needed to continue providing a necessary service for those teens.

DO YOU NEED A MEMORANDUM OF UNDERSTANDING?

A memorandum of understanding (MOU) is a type of agreement between two or more parties. It expresses a convergence of will between the parties, indicating an agreed-upon common course of action. If you're entering a partnership in which each partner must rely on the other, or if there is equipment to be shared between the two partners, an MOU is a good idea. It should outline what each partner is responsible for, and what action will be taken if one member of the partnership doesn't meet their responsibility. The MOU essentially covers both organizations. An MOU can be time-consuming to put together, so usually just one organization (preferably the library) will write it. Then the MOU will go through the library's administration and legal department and will then be shared with the partner organization, and go through a similar review there. There will inevitably be suggestions or edits, which then need to be accepted by both partners. MOUs are excellent tools to outline what each organization is responsible for in a partnership.

EXAMPLE A: PROVIDING OUTREACH SERVICES TO DISADVANTAGED TEENS

Bernie Farrell is the youth services coordinator for the Hennepin County (MN) Library. That library has been providing outreach for teens in collaboration with various partners since the 1990s.

We provide outreach to teens in the following situations:

- Teens who are in a court-ordered residential treatment center.
- Teens in a juvenile detention center, which is a facility for offenders up to age eighteen who have been arrested and are waiting for court disposition or placement.
- Teens at three care and treatment centers: one residential treatment center for adjudicated adolescents; one residential chemical treatment program for adolescent youths with dual diagnosis (mental health and chemical dependency); and a one-day treatment program for adolescent youth with a mental health

diagnosis. These programs are all part of Intermediate District 287, which offers specialized educational programs and services to our twelve-member school districts. These are often specialized services that the member districts individually find it too difficult or costly to provide.

- Teens who are pregnant or parenting.

For pregnant and parenting teens, the Hennepin County Library partners with two local school districts to help the teens develop specific habits that will support early literacy development in their children, and to build the parents' familiarity with and use of library resources that will support their own learning and development. The librarians visit teens enrolled in parenting classes or parent-child together classes once each month from October to May. Each session involves interactive activities based on the needs and interests of the parents enrolled, and includes storytimes, booktalks and book giveaways, "tinkering time" to become familiar with the resources found at hclib.org, and a visit to a nearby branch library.

For teens at all the other locations, the Hennepin County Library provides monthly or bimonthly booktalks, delivers books requested by teens, and provides answers to reference questions. The librarians work together with the teaching staff at each location to help inculcate a culture of reading in the teens. The library has also supported author visits to these sites, including authors such as Nikki Grimes, Angie Thomas, and Lamar Giles.

The library's Outreach Department coordinates most of the outreach to teens, with a team of staff from all over the library system delivering services. The Youth Services Department coordinates the work with pregnant and parenting teens, with a team of staff from libraries near the relevant schools delivering the services to pregnant and parenting teens. A small team of staff at the Minneapolis Central Library intentionally coordinates outreach to the juvenile detention center, since that center is in downtown Minneapolis and many of the teens are also patrons at Minneapolis Central.

Establishing Goals

- For pregnant and parenting teens, the goals are to support these teens in developing specific habits that support early literacy development in their children, and to build their familiarity with and use of library resources that will support their own learning and development.
- For other outreach locations, the goals are to support teens in learning about and choosing books to read for pleasure and/or learning; provide library services in alternative education

environments which do not have access to school libraries; support teaching staff by providing them with access to and information about teen literature; and support teaching staff in their efforts to build a culture of reading. An additional goal is to share information about public libraries and support teens in getting library cards.

Measuring Outreach Efforts

- We measure our outreach efforts in all programs through a combination of surveys—exit surveys given immediately after each outreach event, and surveys asking the teens questions about their reading skills and attitudes before and after participating in the outreach program, as they leave the program or at the end of an academic year. We also do some limited open-ended reflection activities, particularly with the pregnant and parenting teens.
- Through the yearly surveys, and through tracking we provide data on the number and kinds of books that are requested by teens who participate. One of the most successful features of our outreach programs is giving teens the opportunity to learn about books and then request those titles.
- Through the surveys, the teens self-report on the services and the changes in their attitudes about reading and how much they read.
- The staff at the facilities report on the changes they have observed in teens, and their ability to build a "culture of reading" even in situations where teens may be in programs for only a brief time.
- The staff at the facilities report on the value of the library services—particularly the librarian's depth of knowledge of teen literature and her responsiveness to student requests—in supporting their work as educators and therapists.

EXAMPLE B: PROVIDING OUTREACH SERVICES TO TEENS IN SCHOOL SETTINGS

Trixie Dantis is the youth services manager at the Arlington Heights (IL) Memorial Library. She has been providing outreach for seven years.

"Our library staff primarily deliver outreach services to teens in a school setting. By partnering with local schools, we can promote and connect teens with library resources in a place where they are required to be, and in an environment that they are familiar and comfortable with.

"Our staff provide 'traditional' services like booktalks, book discussions, and information literacy and database instruction to support the curriculum. Additionally, we visit high schools monthly to showcase STEM and maker resources: Maker Mondays, Tech Tuesdays, and Workshop Wednesdays. We set up in the school's library, lunchroom, or study hall and engage teens with robotics, DIY projects, engineering challenges, and more.

"Similarly, we visit our high school district's Newcomer Center program, which is a landing place for immigrant teens in the district. This program provides support for newcomer teen students so they can improve their literacy before beginning regular classes in their home school. We facilitate an after-school program there, bringing hands-on projects, often with an aspect that helps the teens to understand American culture. From conversations about Groundhog Day to making yearbooks as the school year comes to an end, we give students a safe place to ask questions about aspects of American culture they might not understand.

"Our school resource bag service fills a need in our community. Often teachers want additional materials to support a theme or assignment in the classroom. The library provides resource bags that can be checked out for six weeks to get more and varied resources into students' hands. The bag includes tech equipment from our Library of Things, like GoPro cameras and Arduinos. This service is especially important at the Newcomer Center and other school buildings where there is no library on-site. At the Newcomer Center, we facilitate a rotating collection of high-interest and native-language items to help foster a love of reading and a positive connection between the library and immigrant students. Often these teens are reading below grade level in their native language, so these materials are important to help build their literacy before they focus on improving their English-language skills.

"For the most part, staff from Teen Services deliver the outreach for teens, with support from their Youth Services colleagues. When subject matter experts would be beneficial, Teen Services staff work with other areas across the library. For example, staff with a focus on early literacy help develop and deliver services to the high school district's teen parents classes. Similarly, Digital Services staff assist with some tech-related events and database instruction.

"There are a couple of classes where we partner with staff from Business Services. One is a quarter-long middle school class, and the other is a year-long high school entrepreneurship class: the students are encouraged to think about a problem they would like to solve or a product they would like to improve. The students are introduced to the resources of the library, including 3D printers for rapid prototyping. Business Services staff highlight databases to help provide the teens with market insight and tools to market their idea or product. The culmination of both classes is a Shark Tank-style presentation by the students.

"Our primary goal for outreach is to connect with and engage teens. Many teens are unaware of the resources the library can offer. By meeting teens where they are, our staff can inform them about our services, and promote them as well. Our staff begin to develop a relationship with teens so that they feel comfortable coming to the library and using its resources.

"I would say the best measure has been seeing our regular monthly visits increase in popularity, and seeing increased interactions month-over-month. Our programs' success is also demonstrated by repeat visitors, by students bringing their friends, and by word-of-mouth promotion.

"We recently started conducting brief, informal surveys with teens at our monthly visits to evaluate services. Their responses inform the types of activities and resources that we bring on future visits. For visits related to specific classes, we try to get a sense of the teens' interests and their desired outcomes at the start of the class, and then we survey them at the end of the class to gauge whether those outcomes had been achieved.

"We keep statistics of interactions for all of our visits: the number of interactions, the number of library cards or reciprocal borrowers registered, and the number of items checked out. We also capture anecdotal information about each visit; the staff fill out a one-page reflection to document how the visit went and if there were ways to improve future visits. We also survey the teachers, school librarians, and other school staff.

"The outreach is done by individual librarians and library staff. Statistics are gathered by age group and are reported to the library board and the state library.

"The programs' impacts are shared with the library board through the public board report prepared each month. The library also designs an annual report that highlights services and other accomplishments during the year, and which is shared with the community. We also highlight our programs' impact on our website, social media, print newsletter, and local newspapers."

THE IMPORTANCE OF EVALUATION

It's critical to evaluate the outreach services you're providing in order to determine their sustainability, and their success or lack of it. By establishing your goals and objectives beforehand, you can evaluate the success of your programs and services based on numbers, surveys, and other tools. You should gather hard data such as attendance figures, numbers of books checked out, and the resources most often used. However, it's also important to collect "soft data" like teen, partner, and staff surveys, as well as anecdotal and reflective information. While outreach services are provided outside of the library, the evaluation of such services is still crucial for the library. All of the services are being provided by the library and should be reported as such.

5

Incorporating Technology into Your Outreach

Creating, developing, and implementing technology programs to share with your outreach partners can help teach digital literacy skills. Digital literacy is the ability to use information and communication technologies to find, evaluate, create, and communicate information, and it involves both cognitive and technical skills. It is a different type of literacy that is important for teens to learn. It cannot be taught just by providing a laptop.

DIGITAL LITERACY SKILLS

Digital literacy requires a variety of strategies and skills, including:

- Critical thinking—questioning how authentic, valid, and useful digital information is
- Communicating and collaborating with others in the digital space
- Utilizing digital tools to design and create compelling original content
- Identifying and using digital tools to effectively access, analyze, use, and share information

There are many different types of technology programs that you can take outside the library and provide to teens. All of these programs should be discussed with your outreach partner before starting, as there may be concerns with bringing in technology to a specific population. For example, some juvenile detention facilities may not provide access to the internet, or may limit their teens' access to it. The steps involved in creating a technology outreach program may include the following ones:

- Write a proposal of what you have in mind, and share it with your library's administration. (This proposal could also be used to apply for a grant to fund the technology program.)
- Share the proposal with your outreach partner. They may have questions about internet use, bandwidth, or how to monitor teens' use of the technology in the program.
- Determine the time commitment for the library staff who will be providing the technology program. Is this program an addition to the outreach already being provided, or is it breaking new ground?
- You may be able to conceive of a technology program, but the implementation may be a different story. Build in the learning of the technology programs, or you may have identified a partner in the providing of said programs.

Newer fluencies like digital literacies are important to teach and make available for teens. These literacies help improve teens' comprehension of information on the internet; their effective use of search engines to find information; their ability to evaluate internet sources; and their ability to communicate using digital communication tools like e-mail, texting, and chat. Digital literacy comprises an array of 21st-century skills that teens can learn now to help take them to the next steps in their schooling or careers.

EXAMPLES OF TECHNOLOGY OUTREACH

Easy Technology Programming

- You can provide laptops in a facility and give library instruction on how to access the library's catalog and databases, as well as online resources like high school courses; streaming book, movie, and music services; driver's license resources; English-language learning; and more.
- If you have access to laptops, tablets, or iPads to bring on the road, there are several software tools that you could download for free.

There are various free software tools that you could download onto laptops and share with your partners. In addition, there are many open-source websites you can access or download that could introduce teens to music creation, 3D design, podcasting, and more. (See the section "Open-Source and Free Software to Download" in the appendix at the end of this book.)

Moderate or More Difficult Programming (in terms of funding)

- You can purchase Kindles and download popular book titles several times a year on them. If you purchase several Kindles, you will be limited to the number of the same title, if you are going to download all of them, as there are licensing issues. A Kindle can provide another medium for accessing books, as well as introducing digital literacy skills.

EXAMPLE: OUTREACH SERVICES IN JUVENILE DETENTION FACILITIES

Teresa Allen is the youth institutions senior consultant for the Colorado State Library.

Teresa advises and supports the library staff in ten state-operated, secure, juvenile detention services centers in Colorado. Most of the staff have little or no library experience and they manage library services part-time, on top of their other job responsibilities. Teresa provides library training by visiting sites and training these staffers at their point of need. She assists staff in selecting materials by giving them access to the online selection lists in Follett Titlewave. She prepares customized collection development plans for each site, so the staff are able to focus on ordering newer, diverse books in fiction and other Dewey ranges. Teresa also encourages and supports the creation and implementation of programming in the juvenile detention sites. She has found that the most successful programs are those where facility staff partner with public library youth services staff to bring in programs with STEM devices, book speed-dating, or the Great Stories Book Club from the American Library Association. A couple of her partnerships have resulted in visits from the best-selling author Simone Elkeles. Some of the services in the detention facilities look very like school or public libraries, but there is a much greater emphasis on safety and security. Teresa also provides an annual full-day mini-conference where she brings together all of the youth institutional library staff across the state, so they can learn from her and from each other.

Bringing Technology Programming into Juvenile Detention Settings

Each juvenile detention facility is different, so first Teresa had to get to know the library staff responsible for implementing the program and make sure they were comfortable with the technology. The library staff was then responsible for getting permission from facility leaders and setting expectations for allowing youth to use the technology. In some instances, Teresa could purchase devices before the program became live, so that staff could get to know the technology first. The biggest concerns were always safety and security. Sometimes a technology program would get going in a facility and then it would be taken away because one or two youths damaged the equipment, or found ways to hurt themselves or others with it. Another limitation was time. Staffs often did not have time to charge and otherwise maintain the devices.

Examples of Technology Programming

Teresa purchased two Launchpads (pre-loaded devices with content for teens) for one of the facilities' library. These devices have educational games and apps. The full-time facility library staff there had those two devices in the hands of youth within a few days of delivery, and the pilot program was so successful that two months later, the library staff requested facility funds to purchase ten more Launchpads.

A purchase of 13 Playaway audiobooks was made for another facility. The part-time library staff there had to negotiate with the facility's leadership for five months to finally get the devices in the hands of the youths. Teresa found that the most successful programs were with pre-loaded devices that do not access the internet; that is, Playaway audiobooks and Launchpads.

YOUR TECHNOLOGY PROGRAMS

Having the ability to provide technology programming to your outreach partners allows their teens to start or expand their 21st-century skills. You should think about ways in which you can provide that learning in the library or by bringing technology onto the road. Sadly, the funding in all libraries may not be robust, so start small and then try to do it right. It is important that the librarians or paraprofessionals who are presenting the technology programs learn all the technologies thoroughly before bringing them on the road.

6

How to Create a Core Collection for Outreach

L ibraries offer much more than books, of course, but providing access to those books, whether digitally or in paperback or hardcover, may be a big part of your partner's expectations. If that is the case, there are several ways in which you can provide book materials.

The teens I have worked with—whether they are in juvenile detention facilities, foster care, are homeless or in transition, or are immigrants or refugees—often say things like: "I want to read books about someone who has been through what I've been through," and "I want to see myself in the pages I'm reading." I have heard these comments so often from teens that they are almost a universal refrain. However, the teens I have worked with have expressed many other wishes, preferences, and aspirations besides the ones just quoted. It is important not to pigeonhole teens and make them one-sided. Accordingly, it is important to develop your collection for all of the populations you're serving, and to always solicit input from the teens you serve.

You should read reviews on new books coming out, use some of the selection tools that are recommended in the appendix, always gather input from teens, elicit comments from your colleagues, and keep a spreadsheet of "possible titles." Then purchase the best of these new titles and clearly mark them as library property. Some of the partners you work with may have rules about bringing in books that are only paperbacks, or they may have questions about the content of some of books. These are concerns that you will need to discuss before building your collection or acquiring new books for it. You should make your title list a living, evolving list. If you are visiting a partner every month and bringing in fifteen titles each time, your list of titles can go quickly. You will have some "core" titles that will always be popular, but you will need to continually build your title list, either by pulling books from your library's existing collection or by purchasing them outright. (For some perennially popular books, see the section "Core Titles for Teen Outreach" in the appendix at the end of this book.)

CREATING COLLECTIONS FOR TEEN FACILITIES

Say you are working with two different organizations; one is a juvenile detention facility, and another is a group home for teens in foster care. You make visits every month, so you're going to be seeing some of the same teens every month. Therefore, you're going to want to bring in fresh and new books often. You may have content limitations, as well as a preferred material type, perhaps only paperbacks. This scenario could present a challenge in terms of what kind material type and content type you are able to provide the teens.

Here's a scenario: you are working with a juvenile detention facility which has 10 units, with approximately 15 teens in each unit. How might you structure your visits? You could bring in 10 different books, having the same 10 for each unit, and booktalk all of them to each unit. You should always ask the teens for their requests on each visit. You may be bringing in 200 books each month; 150 core books that you booktalk and 50 requests that you have filled.

Maybe you are pulling your books from your library's collection. If so, you should create a library account for each facility you visit, to keep track of the materials on that account. Your library may receive a lot of advance reader copies (ARCs), so go through those regularly to see if there are some you could use to create a core collection for the facilities. Does your library have books from a Friends group or donated books that could be of interest and are in good condition? Maybe you could apply for a grant, or you've received funding from a donor to create a collection specifically for one facility. At the Boston Public Library, in our partnership with the Department of Youth Services, we utilized the existing library collection. We created a core collection of 200 books purchased from a grant, added books from the Friends group, and included others from ARCs and additional books from the Collection Development Department. In your library, that department may receive books as

ARCs, they may receive extra copies of books from publishers, and they may receive direct copies from authors or publishers that you could possibly use in creating a collection. You should create a go-to list of titles in your core collection, and then you can keep things fresh by ordering more books based on the requests that teens make. To keep track of all these books we use a spreadsheet with all the titles, and whenever a book is checked out, we record the teen's name and the unit, as well as the month. All of the books are labeled and stamped so they are easy to spot as library property.

If you have a budget to create a collection for your outreach partners, that would be great. If that is the case, make an argument for this budget to be funded each year. With core materials, you can grow your collection by utilizing book reviews and teen input, as well as taking into consideration the specific needs of the partner organization.

DEVELOPING A MOBILE COLLECTION

How do you get to your outreach sites—drive, use public transportation, or walk? You can use any of these modes of transit to bring a collection that is mobile, not cumbersome, and of interest to teens. Paperbacks are a good way to go, since they're not heavy. You could work on compiling a list of titles that you pick from for a year, whether those books are purchased, from the library's collection, from a grant, or from Collection Development. In traveling from site to site, you may be using a car, backpacks for the books, or a cart to go from place to place. If you are using the library's collection, you should create an account for your partner to check books out on, and if you are using your own core collection, you should keep track of the books in a spreadsheet. When you bring books to the outreach site, you may want to create a list of the ones you are bringing, to have some sort of "checkout" list. Teens may use the list to write their names next to the books they would like to check out. This way you can share the list with the partner organization about who checked out what; you're able to keep statistics of what has been checked out; and it gives you a sense of the books that are of interest. This list also becomes a tool to help build your collection. (See the "Sample Book Checkout Sheet" in the appendix.)

To build your core collection, you can use the following methods:

- You could work with the Collection Development Department in taking over some of the ARCs, excess books from publishers, and possibly books that have been weeded from the collection, provided they are of interest and in good condition.
- You can try to obtain a grant. You can seek opportunities like this

on YALSA's website. Maybe your library has some donors who would be interested in funding your collection-building efforts; or your state library association might help, or maybe the Board of Library Commissioners.

- You could reach out to publishers. This may be in the form of a grant request, in which you could lay out what you envision for the collection you're building, and who you're building it for. You should support that vision statement with statistics, goals, and so on.
- The Friends group can also be helpful. You can either utilize their existing collection, or explore the possibility of acquiring some of their funds in order to build up your collection.

EXAMPLE A: USING THE SELECTION PROCESS TO REACH OUT TO THE COMMUNITY

Cindy Hauenstein is the materials selection librarian for the Public Library of Cincinnati and Hamilton County. She works in the Materials Selection and Acquisitions Department.

"I have held my current position since 2012, but have worked for the library for over thirty-one years in a variety of capacities, first as a library assistant and then as a librarian in subject departments and at a branch library. This work gave me the necessary experience and background which have been crucial in my current position as a selection librarian. Most of my career has been spent in an urban setting at the Main Library. During the five years I worked at a branch, I assisted the teen librarian with the collection, programming, and with outreach to the local high schools, including teachers' collections.

"With the Main Library and forty branch locations, our library serves a diverse community, and one of the primary roles of my department is to ensure that we are promoting the library's mission to be a dynamic force in the community, and to meet the needs of the population we serve. Recently, we completed visits to each branch location to meet with staff, discuss how their collection was working, and see if it was meeting the needs of their customers. We examined demographic changes in the area, book clubs that met at the branch, programming, and the need for foreign language and ESL materials. These visits and maintaining open communication between the department, the branches, and the Main Library staff ensure that the collection reflects the community the library serves.

"Although I use standard resources in the selection process such as Baker & Taylor, Ingram, *School Library Journal*, *Booklist*, the *New York Times Book*

Review, Kirkus Reviews, and so on, there are often important works that need to be included in the collection that fall outside of my radar. This is where our customers can play a key role, because through our website, they can suggest materials for the library to purchase. This tool is an invaluable resource for us to reach out to the community, whether the titles are needed for book clubs, or they're titles suggested by local authors who are promoting their own work. Recently, I received a request to purchase a local publication, "We Matter Too." One of the local high schools, Aiken, had started their own publishing venture, Swoop, and this was their first release. Written by the twelfth-grade class, "We Matter Too" highlights the experiences of marginalized groups in our society, and the proceeds from the sale of the book went to help local charities. This was exactly the sort of positive work by our teens that the library wants to promote and encourage.

"In February 2018, one of the librarians in the Teen Department at the Main Library, Emma Willig, started a book club with incarcerated teens at the Hamilton County Youth Center. We are working together to develop a collection for that facility."

EXAMPLE B: REACHING OUT TO TEENAGE GIRLS IN A DETENTION FACILITY

Emma Willig is the teen librarian at the Main Library of the Public Library of Cincinnati and Hamilton County.

"I had no idea what to expect when I first walked into the Hamilton County Juvenile Court Youth Center. Known simply as "the Youth Center," it is an eight-unit, sixteen-pod, county detention facility with 160 secure beds.

"I had a bag full of books and I recruited Antonio Williams, the outreach coordinator for City Council member Jeff Pastor, to go with me. It would just be the two of us and a room full of teenage girls, who probably didn't want to hear what we had to say, in a place that they didn't want to be.

"When we arrived, the Youth Center had a vibe similar to a warehouse. I was asked not to bring any hardback books, paper clips, or papers with staples. At the Center there are no elevator buttons; every door is manually operated by a control room, and an ever-present watchful eye seems to follow every uneasy turn of the hallway.

"I was clutching my bag of paperbacks, and I also carried a handful of colorful bookmarks and a couple of copies of Maya Angelou's poem 'Still I Rise.' I had printed this off at the last minute, remembering the powerful and impactful message of the poem. My only strategy here was that if, for whatever reason, I ran out of words, I would simply rely on Maya's.

"When I entered the room, the girls walked in carrying their chairs, counting off as they crossed the threshold like young soldiers. A clear barrier was drawn for us by the officers in charge. Our table was at the front, and the girls were sitting in rows facing us, just like a classroom. The tension was palpable, and I could tell that they were used to adults coming to lecture them about their life choices.

"I introduced myself and Antonio, and we started asking them some simple questions. Names, ages, if they had ever been to the library, a favorite book they might have, one that they were reading now, had they ever heard of Maya Angelou. Very quickly, the barrier was broken. After thirty minutes, we felt like a group of friends chatting.

"I came to understand the most obvious thing which I should have expected from the beginning: this is a group of teenage girls, with the same emotions, same worries, and same cares that I had when I was their age. School. Family. Relationships. Instagram. Hair. Making money. Trying to stay out of drama.

"Since February, Antonio and I have been going twice a month to the Youth Center, and the mood changes every time. Sometimes the girls are excited, sometimes they are sad, sometimes they want to sit and read, sometimes they want to talk. At times the conversation is extremely deep, at times we spend the whole hour talking about nails and eyelashes. However, one thing remains the same; we always take time to talk about books, poetry, and sometimes an inspirational quote like 'The way you speak to yourself matters.'

"As nervous as I was to make the leap into starting this program, I knew two things: I chose this profession, and I needed to make the most of it. I work at the Main Library in Youth Services. Here is a group of youth that I know don't have equitable access to services. The library stands for equal access for all members of the community, and calls on us to be a dynamic force.

"The information, stories, and relationships that I have built inside the library shouldn't be confined within its four walls. Equal access is equal access. My challenge is to think outside the box for ways to allow library services to reach all corners of our community. Maybe that means I must be a little uncomfortable. That means I get to grow. 'Persistence' and 'resilience' are words the girls and I have talked about at length. Letting our light shine, so that others may do the same.

"I serve my community through the library, using my skills and the abundant resources and support the library offers to give back. The longer that I work here, the more I can provide, and the clearer it becomes to others that the library is a standing monument not only of information, but of service, advocacy, and choice."

THE COLLECTION

Think about the population you'll be working with, and gather direct input from them as to the type and content of the books you should share with them. The collection should speak to them. It's important to remember that it's not a collection you are curating. You are only the facilitator of the collection. Let the teens you are serving curate and create the collection. In that way, the collection you facilitate will be alive and will always be getting better.

Appendix
Resources

The resources in this appendix are meant to help you get started with outreach services. The "Outreach Plan for Teen Librarians" may help in getting you to think of all the beginning pieces. If you believe an MOU may be helpful, there is a good example of one here. When working with an outside partner, you may want to survey the usage of the program/service you are providing; a survey that we used to gather input from teens at a juvenile detention facility is included here. To help expand your ideas of organizations that serve teens, there is a starting list of "National Organizations Serving Teens." There is also a list of some online "Selection Tools" to get ideas for titles; a list of "Core Titles for Teen Outreach" to help you get started in thinking about books of interest to teens; and an annotated list of some booktalks to share with teens. For taking books outside of the library to have them "checked out" by the organization you are working with, there is a "Sample Book Checkout Sheet." There are also resources to help in training staff; advice on how to stay safe in a partner's facility; and an introductory list of free and open-source software to download.

Outreach Plan for Teen Librarians
Memorandum of Understanding (MOU) Example
Restricted Materials for a Juvenile Detention Facility
Survey to Gather Input from Teens in a Juvenile Detention Facility
National Organizations Serving Teens
Selection Tools
Core Titles for Teen Outreach
Booktalks to Hook Teens on Books
Sample Book Checkout Sheet
Staff Training Resources
How to Stay Safe in a Partner's Facility
Open-Source and Free Software to Download

OUTREACH PLAN FOR TEEN LIBRARIANS

- Identify the population.
- Estimate the time commitment for the librarian.
- Describe the need for the library's services and/or programming.
- Describe the programs or services the library will provide.

Goal 1: _____

_____

_____

Outcome: _____

_____

_____

Goal 2: _____

_____

_____

Outcome: _____

_____

_____

Questions to Consider:

- What new service or program will this provide that the library isn't already providing in another way?
- Where will the outreach take place?
- When will the outreach program begin?
- What makes this partnership compelling? What need does it serve? Does it tie in with the library's strategic plan?

MEMORANDUM OF UNDERSTANDING (MOU) EXAMPLE

AGREEMENT:
LIBRARY AND JUVENILE DETENTION FACILITY

DATE: _____

This Agreement is made and entered into by and between the _____ Library, hereinafter referred to as "L," and the juvenile detention facility, hereinafter referred to as "JDF." The Library extends library service to residents of the juvenile detention facility in acknowledgment of the residents' restricted access to public libraries. In providing this service, it is recognized that the informational and recreational needs of residents in institutional settings are balanced against the facility's overall objectives regarding treatment and security. This Agreement covers only those library services provided directly to the juvenile detention facility.

POLICIES

1. This Agreement shall be in effect from _____ through _____.
2. The Teen Services Department of Library (L) will be responsible for providing library services to the JDF. The Teen Librarian will be the staff contact for the Library. _____ will be the primary administrative contact for the JDF.
3. The scope of the collection will restrict those materials that present a threat to the security of the facility and/or the advancement of its treatment programs. Specific focuses have been identified as restricted, and a process has been designed for the facility's staff to request that additional items be removed from the library collection. (See also number 3 under "Restricted Materials for a Juvenile Detention Facility" below.)
4. Materials selected and provided to the JDF as part of the L collection shall meet the cultural, informational, and recreational needs of the residents. Materials will be based on input from the L Teen Librarians, JDF teens, and JDF staff.
5. All books distributed to the JDF will be in paperback.
6. Library cards used to check out materials will have a fine-free status. There will be no charge to the JDF for damaged or lost materials, but JDF staff will make every effort to see that library materials are returned and are in satisfactory condition.
7. A list of the titles of the books will be sent to the JDF representative two weeks before each of the monthly JDF visits.

SERVICES

1. Each month, 10 books will be brought to each unit and will be book-talked, to engage the teens. Then they will have the books for one month. The teens may make requests for additional books. The materials are intended for the use of residents, not staff.
2. L will ensure that teens leaving the JDF will have the opportunity to obtain a library card. Teen Librarians will bring library card applications on each visit and sign up youth who don't have library cards.
3. At least one time during the year, representatives from L will meet with JDF staff to evaluate the service and program.
4. If funding is available, in addition to the monthly booktalks, programs such as a teen summer reading program will be developed by L in conjunction with JDF administration/staff.
5. Each year, L will provide a comprehensive report to the JDF containing an evaluation of the library service and program provided to the JDF.

OTHER

1. Any modifications to the Library services, operations, or functions as described above must be agreed to in writing by both parties.

Juvenile Detention Facility	Library

RESTRICTED MATERIALS FOR A
JUVENILE DETENTION FACILITY

1. The scope of the collection will restrict only those materials that present a threat to the security of the facility and/or the advancement of its treatment programs. The materials listed in number 3 (below) have been deemed by JDF staff as a threat to security or as interfering with the advancement of treatment programs, and thus will not be brought into the facility by L (library) staff. In addition, any materials that are identified by the JDF as not appropriate for distribution will be removed from the collection.
2. The responsibility for monitoring the materials referenced herein primarily rests with JDF staff. However, L staff are expected to be vigilant in ensuring that such materials are not allowed into the school or other areas of the facility.
3. L staff will not distribute any publication or materials determined to be detrimental to the security, good order, or discipline of the JDF. Publications which may not be distributed include, but are not limited to, those which meet one of the following criteria: (a) they depict or describe procedures for the construction or use of weapons, ammunition, bombs, or incendiary devices; (b) they depict, encourage, or describe methods of escape from correctional facilities, or contain blueprints, drawings, or similar descriptions of the same; (c) they depict or describe procedures for the brewing of alcoholic beverages, or the manufacture of drugs; (d) they are written in code; (e) they depict, describe, or encourage activities which may lead to the use of physical violence or group disruption; (f) they encourage or instruct in the commission of criminal activity; (g) they contain sexually explicit material which by its nature or content poses a threat to the security, good order, or discipline of the JDF; (h) any homophobic, pornographic, obscene, or sexually explicit materials or other visual depictions that are harmful to students; (i) materials that use obscene, abusive, profane, lewd, vulgar, rude, inflammatory, threatening, disrespectful, or sexually explicit language; (j) materials that use language or images that are inappropriate in the educational setting or which are disruptive to the educational process; (k) information or materials that could cause damage or danger of disruption to the educational process; (l) materials that use language or images that advocate violence or discrimination toward other people (hate literature) or that may constitute harassment or discrimination or create a serious danger of violence in the facility; (m) materials depicting martial arts; and (n) materials depicting tattooing.
4. Books and materials which have been requested but which are not on the approved list, or have not been previously barred by L, will be reviewed on a case-by-case basis prior to being distributed to residents of the JDF.

SURVEY TO GATHER INPUT FROM TEENS IN A JUVENILE DETENTION FACILITY

1. About how many booktalks have you participated in given by the L at JDF?
   ☐ 1–2
   ☐ 3–4
   ☐ 5–6
   ☐ 7–9
   ☐ 10+

2. How would you describe the booktalks?
   ☐ They are educational
   ☐ They are interesting
   ☐ They are entertaining
   ☐ They present different types of books
   ☐ Other: _____
   _____
   _____

3. Which of these things do you like least about the booktalks?
   ☐ There aren't enough books for us to choose from at the booktalks
   ☐ They don't choose interesting books
   ☐ The booktalks aren't interesting
   ☐ Other: _____
   _____
   _____

4. Have you read books you normally would not have read because of the booktalks?
   ☐ Yes
   ☐ No
   ☐ Don't know

5. During the booktalks we should. . .
   ☐ Cover more books in less detail
   ☐ Cover fewer books in more detail
   ☐ Okay as it is

6. What type of books do you like to hear about the most?
   ☐ Fiction
   ☐ Nonfiction

7. What type of fiction would you like to hear more about?
   ☐ Urban fiction
   ☐ Mystery
   ☐ Fantasy
   ☐ Horror
   ☐ Science fiction
   ☐ Romance
   ☐ Teen fiction
   ☐ Graphic novels
   ☐ Other: _____

   _____

   _____

   _____

8. What type of nonfiction would you like to hear more about?
   ☐ Art
   ☐ Poetry
   ☐ Biography
   ☐ Religion
   ☐ Health
   ☐ Self-help
   ☐ Music
   ☐ Sports
   Other: _____

9. If you could change one thing about the booktalks to improve them, what would it be?

   _____

   _____

   _____

   _____

   _____

NATIONAL ORGANIZATIONS SERVING TEENS

Administration on Children, Youth and Families (ACYF)
www.acf.hhs.gov/acyf (youth in foster care)

This agency oversees major federal programs that support social services which promote the positive growth and development of children, youth, and their families; protective services and shelter for children and youth in at-risk situations; and the adoption of children with special needs.

Advocates for Youth
https://advocatesforyouth.org (youth who are LGBTQI)

Advocates for Youth partners with youth leaders, adult allies, and youth-serving organizations to advocate for policies and champion programs that recognize young people's rights to honest sexual health information; accessible, confidential, and affordable sexual health services; and the resources and opportunities necessary to create sexual health equity for all youth.

Annie E. Casey Foundation
www.aecf.org (youth in foster care)

This charitable foundation is focused on improving the well-being of youth in foster care.

Bridging Refugee Youth and Children's Services.
https://brycs.org (youth who are refugees)

This organization aims to strengthen the capacity of mainstream organizations across the United States to empower and ensure the successful development of refugee children, youth, and their families.

Child Welfare Information Gateway
www.childwelfare.gov

This federally funded information service promotes the safety, permanence, and well-being of children, youth, and families by connecting child welfare, adoption, and other professionals and the public to information, resources, and tools on the topics of child welfare, child abuse and neglect, out-of-home care, adoption, and more. You will find anything having to do with teens in foster care, adoption, or who are suffering abuse at this website.

GLSEN

www.glsen.org (LGBTQI teens)

This organization believes that every student has the right to a safe, supportive, and LGBTQ-inclusive K–12 education. GLSEN is a national network of educators and students, and its local chapters are working to make this right a reality.

Independent Living Skills Program Coordinators

www.childwelfare.gov/organizations/?CWIGFunctionsaction=rols:main.dsp List&rolType=Custom&RS_ID=145 (youth in foster care)

Each U.S. state has a coordinator that works directly with youth who are aging out of foster care.

McKinney-Vento Act

www.doe.mass.edu/mv (youth who may be homeless)

This federal law provides funds for homeless shelter programs. Its special focus is on maintaining a network of statewide homeless coordinators who work with and make sure that children and youth who are experiencing homelessness attend school.

National Coalition for Homeless Youth

www.nn4youth.org/engage/nchy (youth who may be homeless)

This coalition facilitates communication and collaboration among the organizations that are working to address youth homelessness, or which are working on issues that intersect with youth homelessness.

Office of Juvenile Justice and Delinquency Prevention

www.ojjdp.gov (teens who are incarcerated)

This federal office works to prevent juvenile delinquency, improve the juvenile justice system, and protect youth.

SELECTION TOOLS

American Indian Youth Literature Award
https://ailanet.org/activities/american-indian-youth-literature-award

Awarded biennially, this award identifies and honors the very best writing and illustrations by and about Native Americans and Indigenous peoples of North America.

Diversity in YA
www.diversityinya.com

This website has a great compilation of diverse teen books and a blog with reviews and write-ups on books.

New York Public Library
www.nypl.org/voices/blogs/blog-channels/sta

For eighty years this library has had Books for the Teen Age, which has now become Stuff for the Teen Age. It's a blog channel about the best of the year in teen books, music, graphic novels, movies, games, and more.

Orca Publishers
www.orcabook.com

Orca offers five different series of high-interest, low-reading level (hi-lo) fiction for those readers facing literacy issues. The series are Orca Currents, Orca Sports, Orca Limelights, Orca Soundings, and Rapid Reads.

The Pirate Tree
www.thepiratetree.com

This is a collective of children's and young adult writers who are interested in children's literature and social justice issues.

School Library Journal
www.slj.com

This well-known journal has book reviews and write-ups by genres.

Social Justice Books
https://socialjusticebooks.org/booklists

This website offers more than sixty carefully selected lists of multicultural and social justice books for children, young adults, and educators.

We Need Diverse Books

https://diversebooks.org

This website has a great starting list of diverse books that is continually updated. It also has a helpful booktalking kit.

YALSA booklists

www.ala.org/yalsa/booklistsawards/booklistsyield

The YALSA website has lists of great titles like Great Graphic Novels, Quick Picks, and Popular Paperbacks.

You can also reach out to other teen librarians who are doing outreach and ask them what resources and titles they use to build their collections.

CORE TITLES FOR TEEN OUTREACH

Here are some core titles that are widely relevant and perennially popular with teens.

Always Running: La Vida Loca: Gang Days in LA (1993).
Bronxwood (2011). The sequel to *Tyrell*.
Coldest Winter Ever (1999).
The 48 Laws of Power (1998).
The Hate U Give (2017).
Monster: A Graphic Novel (2015).
My Bloody Life: The Making of a Latin King (2000).
Once a King, Always a King: The Unmaking of a Latin King (2004).
The New Jim Crow: Mass Incarceration in the Age of Colorblindness (2010).
No Choirboy: Murder, Violence, and Teenagers on Death Row (2008).
Perfect Chemistry (2008). The first novel in a trilogy.
The Rose That Grew from Concrete (2009).
Speak: The Graphic Novel (2019).
Tyrell (2010).

BOOKTALKS TO HOOK TEENS ON BOOKS

A booktalk is not a review of the book; rather, it's a way to give just enough of the book away to hook the reader. Think of it as an advertisement for the book, and you're trying to sell the book to customers. While it helps to have read the book that you're doing a booktalk about, sometimes this is just not possible. A lot of authorities and websites on booktalks will say that you should read the read before booktalking it. I think it's possible to do a booktalk without reading the book first.

Some of the book descriptions in your library's catalog or on Amazon can be helpful in providing a synopsis of the book. They can give you an overview of the book and bullet words that help with describing its content. If you're talking about twenty different books, how might you structure the booktalks? You could give ten one-minute booktalks in which you give short overviews of each of the books, focusing on their major themes. Maybe five of the books are like the ones you already introduced, and then with the last five you could go into more detail, so the talks are three minutes for each book. I think you can talk about books you may not like and that you may not have read. But you really must do your homework by getting an idea of what the book is about, its major themes, and the characters.

The Alchemist by Paul Coelho.
Bait by Alex Sanchez.
Midnight by Sister Souljah.
The Sneaker Book by Tom Vanderbilt.
Street Pharm by Allison Van Diepen.
Ten Mile River by Paul Griffin.

SAMPLE BOOK CHECKOUT SHEET

Spanish Books––December 20 Number of teens:

Name of Teen	Unit	Title, Author	Barcode
		Camino Cruzados – Ally Condie	39999XXXXXXXXX
		Francisco: El Primer Papa Latino Americano – Mario Escobar	39999XXXXXXXXX
		Hasta Martes – Luis Carlos Montalvan	39999XXXXXXXXX
		La Ley 50 – 50 Cent	39999XXXXXXXXX
		Me Llamo Neymar – Mauro Beting and Ivan More	39999XXXXXXXXX
		El Engaño de Bourne – Eric Lustbader	39999XXXXXXXXX
		Los Juegos del Hambre – Suzanne Collins	39999XXXXXXXXX
		Mi Hijo Precioso – David Sheff	39999XXXXXXXXX
		El Hobbit – J. R. R. Tolkien	39999XXXXXXXXX
		La Breve y Maravillosa Vida de Oscar Wao – Junot Diaz	39999XXXXXXXXX

STAFF TRAINING RESOURCES

Trainings can help provide you with an overview of the challenges that may face some teen populations, as well as offer you ways in which to work with those teens. It may be difficult to participate in some trainings, since there may be a cost, unless your library is supporting those trainings financially. Some of the training you participate in could be reading and research into organizations that work with and support those youth.

Here are some organizations and other resources to consider:

GENERAL RESOURCES

Annie E. Casey Foundation
www.aecf.org (help for working with youth in foster care)

This foundation strengthens families, builds stronger communities, and ensures access to opportunity, because youth need all three to succeed. The foundation provides solutions to overcome the barriers to success for youth in foster care. Reading some of the data and articles about youth in care gives you a solid sense of some of their barriers and challenges.

Child Welfare Information Gateway
www.childwelfare.gov (help for working with youth who are immigrants and/or refugees)

This is a federal government website that provides information for professionals working with immigrant youth or refugees, including help in navigating the legal issues commonly faced by these young people.

Library Services for Youth in Custody
(help for working with youth who are incarcerated)

This is an ALA interest group that serves the needs of, and advocates for, those libraries which provide services to youth in custody. Those "in custody" would include, at the least, incarcerated, detained, or committed youth in both juvenile and adult settings in municipal, county, local, state, or federal facilities, including ICE detention centers and youth in secure mental health or rehab settings. Those "in custody" might also include at-risk youth in other forms of group housing or government custody. There are several resources included in this agency that focus on collection development, discussions about working with teens who are incarcerated, continuing education, and more.

National Mentoring Resource Center

https://nationalmentoringresourcecenter.org (help for working with youth who are or were incarcerated)

This center supports mentoring opportunities for youth who have been arrested or incarcerated. Mentoring is a widely used prevention and intervention strategy for supporting youth who are involved in the criminal justice system. The center's website provides several resources, including webinars to provide tips specific to mentoring young people who are involved in the juvenile justice system.

National Network for Youth (NN4Y)

www.nn4youth.org (help for working with youth who may be homeless or in transition)

The NN4Y been a public education and policy advocacy organization dedicated to the prevention and eradication of youth homelessness in America for over forty years. They provide several resources that can help give you a sense of how youth become homeless, how youth homelessness can be prevented, and ways in which to do so.

Office of Diversity, Literacy, and Outreach Services

www.ala.org/aboutala/offices/diversity

This ALA office offers continuing education, e-learning, workshops, presentations, webinars, and consultations for librarians who are working with and supporting underserved populations.

Yalsa-lockdown discussion list

yalsa-lockdown@lists.al.org (help for working with youth who are incarcerated)

Think about joining the YALSA-lockdown discussion list, which discusses issues unique to librarians working with incarcerated youth.

YOUTH MENTAL HEALTH TRAINING

Mental Health First Aid

www.mentalhealthfirstaid.org

This is a training course that teaches participants how to spot people who are suffering from mental health or substance-use issues. The course provides good information, but there is a fee associated with the training.

GLSEN (Gay Lesbian & Straight Education Network)

www.glsen.org

This national organization has chapters in all fifty states and provides trainings on anti-LGBT bias and harassment, LGBTQ competency, and ways to effectively intervene when you see or hear bullying take place. There is a cost to their trainings.

TRAUMA-INFORMED CARE TRAINING

My Brother's Keeper Alliance

www.mentoring.org/program-resources/my-brothers-keeper-webinars/#1455132 514364-e258ecdf-2130

Webinars and virtual trainings through the Alliance focus on looking at race and privilege and looking at ways to mentor young men of color.

You may also be able to find trainings through your city's Public Health Commission.

HOW TO STAY SAFE IN A PARTNER'S FACILITY

- Know the rules of the facility in which you are working and follow those rules.
- Don't allow yourself to be alone with a teen. Make sure there are always staff and other teens present. This is to protect yourself, as well as the teen.
- Don't share personal information about yourself with teens. You want to be friendly, but you don't need to share what neighborhood you live in, or if you are not married.
- Know the facility's dress code; what not to wear.
- Be a friendly, supportive, and positive adult to the teens you work with, and that means *all* of the teens. Don't have favorites, or treat any teen different than the others.

OPEN-SOURCE AND FREE SOFTWARE TO DOWNLOAD

Audacity
https://sourceforge.net/projects/audacity

This is a free, easy-to-use, multitrack audio editor and recorder for Windows, Mac OS X, GNU/Linux, and other operating systems. It's great for music creation programs.

Blender
blender.org

This is an open-source 3D creation site. It includes tutorials to help you learn how to use the site.

Inkscape
inkscape.org

This has professional-quality vector graphics software which runs on Windows, Mac OS X and GNU/Linux. It's comparable to Adobe Illustrator, and includes tutorials.

Podbean
Podbean.com

This is an easy, free way to start podcasting.

qStopMotion
qStopMotion.org

This is a free application for creating stop-motion animation movies.

Scratch
https://scratch.mit.edu

This teaches beginning coding, and you can program your own interactive stories, games, and animations—and share your creations with others in the online community. It includes resources for educators and librarians to learn to prepare and run Scratch classes and workshops.

Tinkercad
tinkercad.com

This is an easy-to-use 3D CAD design tool. It includes tutorials and lessons you may use to teach others how to create on Tinkercad.

Index

A

Administration on Children, Youth and Families (ACYF), 68
advance reader copies (ARCs), 54, 55
advocacy, 4–8
Advocates for Youth, 68
Alameda County (CA) Library Juvenile Hall, 17
The Alchemist (Coelho), 73
alcohol and drug recovery schools, 14–15
Allen, Teresa, 51–52
alternative schools
  alcohol and drug recovery schools, 14–15
  description of, 14
  overview of, 18
American Indian Youth Literature Award, 70
American Library Association (ALA), 1, 3
Angelou, Maya, 57, 58
Annie E. Casey Foundation, 68, 75
ARCs (advance reader copies), 54, 55
Arlington Heights (IL) Memorial Library, 46–48
assessment
  See evaluation
Audacity, 79

B

Bait (Sanchez), 73
barriers, 4–5

Belpré, Pura, 3–4
Bernier, Anthony, vii–viii
BFI (Bureau of Fearless Ideas), 24–25
bicycles, 38
Bisson, Jennifer, 23–25
Black Americans, 3
Blender, 79
book requests, 42
bookmobiles, 2–3
books
  collections for teen facilities, 54–55
  core collection for outreach, 53–54
  for mobile collection, 55–56
  outreach services for incarcerated teens, xii–xiii
  for outreach to girls in detention facility, 57–58
  Sample Book Checkout Sheet, 74
  selection process for community outreach, 56–57
booktalk
  Booktalks to Hook Teens on Books, 73
  by Hennepin County Library, 45
  at juvenile detention facility, 54
Booktalks to Hook Teens on Books, 61, 73
Boston Public Library (BPL)
  collection for teen facilities, 54–55
  internship program in Teen Central, 31–33
  Jess Snow''s outreach work at, xi–xiii

Boston Public Library (BPL) *(cont'd)*
  library staff, involvement in outreach,
    8–9
  partnerships with juvenile detention
    centers, 17
Boy Scouts, 35
Boys and Girls Clubs, 23–24
Bridging Refugee Youth and Children"s
    Services, 68
Brooklyn Public Library (BPL), 5, 17
budget, 55
Bureau of Fearless Ideas (BFI), 24–25

C

Charlotte Mecklenburg (NC) Public
    Library
  outreach program of, 34–36
  partnerships with juvenile detention
    centers, 17
  role of staff in providing outreach,
    34–36
checkout sheet
  for mobile collection, 55
  Sample Book Checkout Sheet, 74
Child Welfare Information Gateway, 68,
    75
Civil Rights Act, 1964, 2
Coelho, Paulo, 73
collaboration, 35, 49
  See also partnerships
collection
  Core Titles for Teen Outreach, 72
  input from teens for, 59
  mobile collection, 55–56
  for outreach, development of, 53–54
  outreach to teenage girls in detention
    facility, 57–58
  Restricted Materials for Juvenile
    Detention Facility, 65
  selection process to reach out to
    community, 56–57
  for teen facilities, 54–55
Collection Development Department, 55
Colorado State Library, 51–52
Committee on Library Extension, ALA, 3
communication
  as digital literacy skill, 49
  for lasting partnership, 22–23

community
  Charlotte Mecklenburg Public Library"s
    outreach program and, 34–36
  demographics of, 6
  Oakland Public Library"s outreach
    services and, 36–38
  outreach services, need for, 5–6
  selection process for community
    outreach, 56–57
  selection process to reach out to, 56–57
  social services organizations, 6–7
  understanding of, 9
community organizations
  Greenwood Branch of Seattle Public
    Library"s partnership with, 23–25
  Johnson County Library"s
    partnerships with, 25–28
consistency, 28
content creation, 49
Core Titles for Teen Outreach, 61, 72
CORI-cleared (Criminal Offender Record
    Information), 21
counseling services, 18
critical thinking, 49
cultural awareness, 38
cultural competence, 34
curriculum, 33

D

Dantis, Trixie, 46–48
data collection, 43, 48
day centers for previously court-involved
    youth, 14
demographics
  of community, examination of, 6
  teen demographic for outreach, 21–22
Department of Children and Families
    (DCF), 13
Department of Youth Services (DYS)
  collection for teen facilities, 54–55
  Jess Snow"s partnership with, xi–xiii
  outreach plan for partnership with,
    8–9
digital literacy
  skills for, 49
  technology programs for, 50–52
digital tools, 49
diversity, 34, 38

Diversity in YA, 70
drug recovery schools, 14–15
DYS
  See Department of Youth Services

E
EDCO Collaborative, 19
Elkeles, Simone, 51
emergency shelters, 12
evaluation
  of impact of outreach services, 43
  importance of, 48
  of outreach efforts, 46
exit surveys, 46
expectations, 23

F
facility policies, 19–20
Farrell, Bernie, 44–46
federal programs, 18–19
feedback
  See input
foster care
  collection for group home, creation of,
    54–55
  foster homes, 12–13
  ILSP for youth in, 6, 13
  liaison for foster youth, 19
Fostering Connections to Success and
    Increasing Adoptions Act of 2008,
    13, 19
Four Corners Mobile Library Project, 3
Friends group, 56
funding
  for collection for teen facilities,
    54–55
  for homeless youth programs, 18
*The Future of Library Services for and with
    Teens: A Call to Action* (YALSA), 34

G
gender, 15
girls
  in juvenile justice system, 14
  outreach to girls in detention facility,
    57–58
GLSEN (Gay Lesbian & Straight Education
    Network), 69, 77

goals
  for internship program, 32
  for partnership, 22–23
goals/outcomes for outreach services
  evaluation of impact of outreach
    services, 43
  evaluation of outreach services,
    importance of, 48
  examples of goals, 42
  for improvement of outreach services,
    43–44
  memorandum of understanding, 44
  for outreach services, 41–42
  outreach services to disadvantaged
    teens, 44–46
  outreach services to teens in school
    settings, 46–48
grant, 55–56
Greenwood Branch of Seattle Public
    Library, 23–25
Griffin, Paul, 73
group homes, 13, 16–17

H
Hamilton County Juvenile Court Youth
    Center, 57–58
Hauenstein, Cindy, 56–57
Hennepin County (MN) Public Library
  outreach services of, 8
  outreach services to disadvantaged
    teens, 44–46
  partnerships with juvenile detention
    centers, 17
homeless shelters
  description of, 12
  McKinney-Vento Act provides federal
    funding for, 18
  for teens, overview of, 16
homeless youth
  federal programs to assist, 18
  homeless shelters for, 12
  outreach services goal for, 42
  social services organizations and, 6–7
  unaccompanied youth, 4
How to Stay Safe in a Partner"s Facility, 78

I
immigrant youth, 15, 19

incarcerated teens
    Jess Snow"s outreach work with, xi–xiv
    library staff for outreach services and, 9
    See also juvenile detention facilities
Independent Living Skills Program (ILSP)
    description of, 13
    Independent Living Skills Program Coordinators, 6, 69
    overview of, 17
Indian Self-Determination and Education Assistance Act, 3
Inkscape, 79
input
    from community for selection process, 57
    Survey to Gather Input from Teens in a Juvenile Detention Facility, 66–67
    from teens about collection, 53, 59
internet, 50
interns, 32
internship program, 31–33

J

job description, of teen librarian, 30
Johnson County Juvenile Detention Center, 25–26
Johnson County (KS) Public Library
    partnerships with community organizations, 25–26
    partnerships with juvenile detention centers, 17
    program overview, 27–28
Jones, Patrick, 8
juvenile court, 14
juvenile detention facilities
    collection for, 54–55
    description of, 14
    Johnson County Library"s partnership with, 25–26
    outreach to teenage girls in, 57–58
    overview of, 17
    policies of, following, 20
    Restricted Materials for Juvenile Detention Facility, 65
    staff training resources, 75
    Survey to Gather Input from Teens in a Juvenile Detention Facility, 66–67
    technology outreach services in, 50, 51–52
juvenile justice system, 37

K

Kindles, 51

L

laptop
    in juvenile detention center library program, 26
    for technology outreach program, 50–51
lasting partnership, 22–23
Launchpads, 52
learning, 50
Learning Buddies program, 24
LGBTQIA youth
    in juvenile justice system, 14
    library outreach services, need for, 15
    organizations for, 19
liaison, 19
librarian
    cultural awareness of, 38
    diversity among, 34
    policies of youth facilities, following, 19–20
    See also teen librarian
library
    internship program, potential benefits of, 32
    library programs/services in partner"s facility, 21
    outreach, library staff involvement in, 8–9
    outreach services, history of, 2–4
    partnership with youth facilities, 19–20
library cards, xiii
Library ETC (Explore, Tinker, Connect) program, 26
library patrons, 4–8
Library Services for Youth in Custody, 75
library staff
    Charlotte Mecklenburg Public Library example, 34–36
    cultural awareness of, 38
    diversity among, 34

internship program in outreach
services, 31–33
Oakland Public Library example, 36–38
Staff Training Resources, 75–77
teen librarian, characteristics of, 29–30
teen librarian job description, 30–31
teen outreach services, involvement
in, 8–9
"local education liaisons," 6

M

McCarter, Pamela, 34–36
McIntosh, Peggy, 34
McKellar, Sharon, 36–38
McKinney-Vento Homeless Education
Assistance Act
funding for homeless youth programs,
18
link for, 69
requirements of, 6–7
McNair, Kate, 25–28
memorandum of understanding (MOU)
example of, 61, 63–64
importance of, 44
for outreach program, xii, xiii
for partnership, 22–23
for partnership with youth facility, 21
policies included in, 20
mental health, 76–77
Mental Health First Aid, 76
Midnight (Souljah), 73
Migrant Education Program, 19
mission, 12
mobile collection, 55–56
mobile library, 2–4
mobility, 5
MOU
See memorandum of understanding
My Brother"s Keeper Alliance, 77

N

National Coalition for Homeless Youth, 69
National Indian Omnibus Library Bill, 3
National Mentoring Resource Center, 76
National Network for Youth (NN4Y), 76
National Organizations Serving Teens, 61,
68–69
Native Americans, 3

New York Public Library (NYPL)
library outreach services of, 3–4, 5
partnerships with juvenile detention
centers, 17
selection tools of, 70
Newcomer Center program, 47

O

Oakland Public Library (CA), 36–38
objectives, 41
Office for Diversity, Literacy, and Outreach
Services (ODLOS), 1, 7, 76
Office for Refugees and Immigrants, 15
Office of Juvenile Justice and Delinquency
Prevention, 69
115th Street Branch Library, 3–4
Open-Source and Free Software to
Download, 61, 79
open-source websites, 51
Orca Publishers, 70
organizations
community organizations, 23–28
national organizations serving teens,
68–69
reaching out to, in partnership
creation, 11–12
for staff training resources, 75–77
youth facilities, types of, 12–15
outcomes
See goals/outcomes for outreach
services
outreach
core collection for, creation of, 53–59
creativity with definition of, 7
definition of, 1
Jess Snow"s work in teen services,
xi–xiv
role of staff in providing, 29–38
service power with, vii–viii
technology programs, 49–52
in teen librarian job description, 30–31
Outreach Plan for Teen Librarians, 61, 62
outreach services
advocating for, 4–8
definition of, need for, xiii–xiv
first steps for providing, 5–7
goals for continuous improvement of,
43–44

outreach services *(cont'd)*
    history of, 2–4
    impact of, evaluation of, 43
    library staff involvement in, 8–9
    partnerships, creating, 11–12
    partnerships, youth facilities to
      partner with, 12–15
    principles to apply, 7–8
    x, 41–48
    youth facilities, nuts/bolts of, 16–18
Outreach Services for Teens (Snow)
    Anthony Bernier on, vii–viii
    introduction to, xiii–xiv
outreach training retreat, 35–36
outside partners, 28

P

paperbacks
    for collections for teen facilities, 54
    for juvenile detention center outreach,
      57
    for mobile collection, 55
parents
    Hennepin County Library"s outreach
      to teen parents, 45–46
    young parent programs, partnership
      with, 19
    young parents, organizations that
      serve, 15
partnerships
    alternative schools, 18
    with community organizations, 23–28
    creating, 11–12
    with DYS, 8–9
    facility policies, following, 19–21
    federal/other programs to assist youth,
      18–19
    group homes, 16–17
    homeless shelters, 16
    How to Stay Safe in a Partner"s Facility,
      78
    Independent Living Skills Programs, 17
    for internship program in outreach
      services, 31–33
    juvenile detention centers, 17
    lasting partnership, keys to, 22–23
    library programs/services in partner"s
      facility, 21

memorandum of understanding for,
    44, 63–64
for Oakland Public Library"s outreach,
    37
outside partners, working with, 28
technology outreach program proposal
    and, 50
in teen librarian job description, 30
teens you might work with, 21–22
youth facilities, types of, 12–15
People"s Free Library, Chester County,
    South Carolina, 2
performance evaluation, 31
plan, Outreach Plan for Teen Librarians,
    62
Playaway audiobooks, 52
Podbean, 79
Point in Time Estimates of Homelessness,
    4
policies, of youth facilities, 19–20
poverty, 5
pregnancy, 45–46
principles, 7–8
proposal
    for outreach program, xii, 8–9
    for technology outreach program, 50
public libraries, 17
Public Library of Cincinnati and Hamilton
    County
    outreach to teen girls in detention
      facility, 57–58
    selection process for community
      outreach, 56–57
publishers, 56
Puerto Ricans, 3–4

Q

qStopMotion, 79

R

readers, 15
reading
    culture of, 45
    measurement of outreach efforts,
      46
    at Newcomer Center, 47
refugee teens
    organizations that work with, 15

partnership with organizations serving, 19
report
  on goals/outcomes of partnership, 22–23
  on outreach services, 7
residential facilities, 13
resource guides, 36
resources
  Booktalks to Hook Teens on Books, 73
  Core Titles for Teen Outreach, 72
  How to Stay Safe in a Partner"s Facility, 78
  Memorandum of Understanding (MOU) example, 63–64
  National Organizations Serving Teens, 68–69
  Open-Source and Free Software to Download, 79
  Outreach Plan for Teen Librarians, 62
  overview of, 61
  Restricted Materials for Juvenile Detention Facility, 65
  Sample Book Checkout Sheet, 74
  for selection process, 56–57
  selection tools, 70–71
  Staff Training Resources, 75–77
  Survey to Gather Input from Teens in a Juvenile Detention Facility, 66–67
responsibilities, 23, 44
Restricted Materials for Juvenile Detention Facility, 61, 65
reviews, 53

S
safety
  How to Stay Safe in a Partner"s Facility, 78
  policies of youth facilities, following, 20
  technology in juvenile detention facilities and, 52
safety net hospital, 43
Sample Book Checkout Sheet, 61, 74
Sanchez, Alex, 73
School Library Journal, 70
school resource bag service, 47

schools
  homeless youth and, 18
  Oakland Public Library"s outreach work with, 37
  outreach services to teens in school settings, 46–48
Scratch, 79
Seattle Public Library, 23–25
selection
  collection selection process for community outreach, 56–57
  tools, list of, 70–71
Selection Tools resource, 61, 70–71
sexual orientation, 15
"Share the Love" collection, 38
shelters
  See homeless shelters
Simmons University, 31
SketchUp, 26, 27–28
skills
  digital literacy skills, 49
  goal for learning, 42
The Sneaker Book (Vanderbilt), 73
Snow, Jess
  Anthony Bernier on *Outreach Services for Teens*, vii–viii
  outreach work of, xi–xiv
social services organizations, 6–7
SocialJusticeBooks.org, 70
software
  Open-Source and Free Software to Download, 79
  for technology outreach program, 50–51
Souljah, Sister, 73
South Bronx Library Program, 4
spreadsheet
  for collection for teen facilities, 55
  for mobile collection, 55
  for "possible titles" for collection, 53
  Sample Book Checkout Sheet, 74
staff
  See library staff
staff members, of youth facility, 21
Staff Training Resources, 61, 75–77
stakeholders, 8
statewide homeless coordinator, 6
"Still I Rise" (Angelou), 57

strategic plan, 5–6
Street Pharm (Van Diepen), 73
Survey to Gather Input from Teens in a
  Juvenile Detention Facility, 61,
  66–67
surveys
  for assessment of outreach services,
    46, 48
  for teens participating in outreach
    program, xiii
sustainability, of partnership, 12

T
technology
  digital literacy skills, 49–50
  in juvenile detention center, 26
  outreach programs, examples of, 50–52
  your technology programs, 52
Teen Central of the Boston Public Library,
  31–33
teen facilities, collection for, 54–55
teen librarian
  in BPL outreach program, xiii
  characteristics of, 29–30
  job description, 30–31
  Outreach Plan for Teen Librarians, 62
  Outreach Services for Teens (Snow) for,
    xiii–xiv
teen outreach services
  advocating for, 4–8
  Core Titles for Teen Outreach, 72
  facility policies, following, 19–20
  goals/outcomes for, 41–48
  Jess Snow''s outreach work, xi–xiv
  outreach to teen girls in detention
    facility, 57–58
  partnerships, creating, 11–12
  selection process for community
    outreach, 56–57
  teen demographic for outreach, 21–22
  youth facilities, nuts/bolts of, 16–18
  youth facilities to partner with, 12–15
teens
  collection development and, 53
  collections for teen facilities, 54–55
  digital literacies and, 50

input about collection from, 59
National Organizations Serving Teens,
  68–69
outreach services to disadvantaged
  teens, 44–46
outreach services to teens in school
  settings, 46–48
Survey to Gather Input from Teens in a
  Juvenile Detention Facility, 66–67
teen demographic for outreach,
  21–22
youth facilities, nuts/bolts of, 16–18
youth facilities, types of, 12–15
Ten Mile River (Griffin), 73
The Pirate Tree, 70
3D Mashup program
  overview of, 27–28
  template for, 26
time commitment, 11, 50
Tinkercad, 79
Titcomb, Mary Lemist, 2
titles
  collection selection process for
    community outreach, 56–57
  Core Titles for Teen Outreach, 72
  list of for mobile collection, 55
training
  in internship program, 31–33
  Staff Training Resources, 75–77
transportation
  as barrier for teen patrons, 5
  of library outreach materials, 21
  mobile collection and, 55
trauma-informed care training, 77

U
underserved populations
  diversity among librarians and, 34
  history of outreach services to, 2–4
  social services organizations and, 6–7
United We Dream, 15

V
Van Diepen, Allison, 73
Vanderbilt, Tom, 73
vision, 32

W

Washington County Free Library,
    Hagerstown, Maryland, 2
"We Matter Too" publication, 57
We Need Diverse Books, 71
White House Pre-Conference on Indian
    Library and Information Services
    on or Near Reservations, 3
White privilege, 34
"White Privilege: Unpacking the Invisible
    Knapsack" (McIntosh), 34
Williams, Antonio, 57–58
Willig, Emma, 57–58
Works Progress Administration, 2
Works Projects Administration, 3

Y

Young Adult Library Services Association
    (YALSA)
    booklists of, 71
    on characteristics of teen librarian,
        29–30
    on cultural competence, 34
    grant information on website of, 56
    Yalsa-lockdown discussion list,
        76

youth
    federal programs to assist, 18–19
    mental health training resources, 76–77
    teen outreach services, advocating for,
        4–8
    See also homeless youth; teens
youth facilities
    alcohol and drug recovery schools,
        14–15
    alternative schools, 14, 18
    day centers for previously court-
        involved youth, 14
    foster homes, 12–13
    group homes, 13, 16–17
    homeless shelters, 12, 16
    immigrant/refugee teens,
        organizations that work with, 15
    Independent Living Skills Program,
        13, 17
    juvenile detention centers, 14, 17
    library programs/services in partner"s
        facility, 21
    policies, following, 19–20
    residential facilities, 13
    types of, 12–15
youth.gov, 6